慈鯛科•CICHLIDEN

CICHLIDS

The Pictorial Guide

Volume One

Pablo Tepoot & Ian M. Tepoot

Revised & Updated Edition

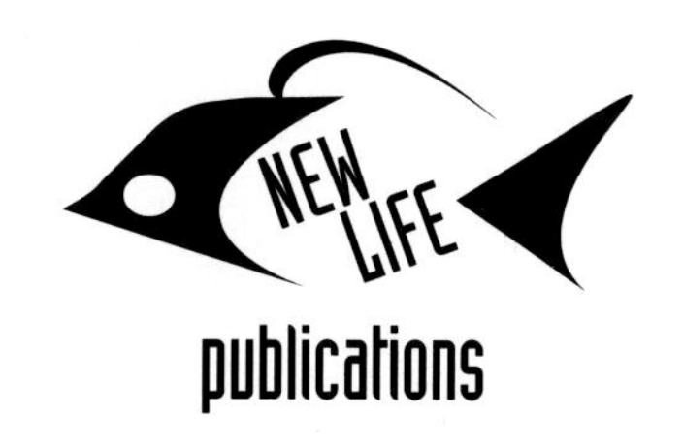

A Subsidiary of New Life Exotic Fish, Inc.

CICHLIDS: The Pictorial Guide

1st printing March 1995.
2nd printing June 1995.

Published by
New Life Publications
25855 S.W. 193 Ave.
Homestead, Fl. 33031
Tel : (305) 245-2404
Fax : (305) 248-7450

ISBN 0-9645058-0-0

Printed in Hong Kong

ACKNOWLEDGMENTS

Dedicated To Linda L. Tepoot

Dr. Harry Grier's photographic techniques were adapted by the authors when photographing the cichlids pictured in this book. Without his expertise, publishing this book would have been a much more difficult task.

Thanks to Annette Bentler, who translated the *preface* into German.

Finally, thanks to Sophie Lee, who proofread the Chinese text, and Windy Y. Lawrence—who did the same for the English version.

PREFACE

The basic goals of this book can be stated in three words: *clarity, clarity* and *clarity*. Unfortunately, this is a rare commodity when dealing with cichlids. Most industries or professions have a common ground of names and terms that allow them to communicate clearly with each other without resorting to the most simian sorts of shenanigans. Unfortunately, within the world of cichlids, this common ground is shaky, to say the least.

Since the early 70's, when African Cichlids began to become widely available to dealers and hobbyists, new fish have been discovered and made available to consumers at an astounding rate. This relentless pace has outstripped the scientists' ability to classify and name the fish. The result has been a virtual Tower of Babel, consisting of a jumble of sporadic and inconsistent names.

This lack of a truly definitive taxonomy has left a vacuum, into which has grown a wild jungle of non–uniform common names and strange sets of scientific/common name hybrids based on "best guess" classifications.

There are two basic oddities in this idiosyncratic name system: the *many fish with one name* and the *many names for one fish* syndromes. The first situation, many fish with one name, is illustrated beautifully by *Aulonocara stuart-granti*. This name has been applied to *three* visually distinct fish: the *Mbenji Peacock, Ngara Peacock* and *Flavescens Peacock*. Situations such as this add to the already difficult task of speaking about and listing fish clearly and precisely.

The second "syndrome"—giving one fish many names—applies to virtually every cichlid. Rarely do you find a specimen that *doesn't* have several names. Often these consist of a "scientific name", a few common names and a series of names which are strange combinations of both.

Cichlid names are subject to frequent changes in classification. As these classifications shift, each book published on cichlids tends to pick one system of names it favors, to the exclusion of the others. The problem with this, predictably, is that if the reader does not happen to be familiar with that system, finding what you want is a definite problem.

One good example of this was the classification of a wide variety of fish into the genus *Haplochromis* for the sake of simplicity. However, once this became firmly entrenched, *Haplochromis* was again broken down into the older genus classifications such as *Dimidiochromis, Copadichromis* and *Sciaenochromis*.

This inconsistency, coupled with regional differences (such as those between Europe & the U.S.), further erodes the precious common ground we rely on for clear, reliable communication within the cichlid community.

All of these difficulties lead us back, quite conveniently, to the purpose of the book: *clarity*. The philosophy behind this book is based on a need in the industry for a photo ref-erence guide to cichlids which puts emphasis on the clear, concise presentation of information.

A picture, the old cliché tells us, is worth a thousand words. This is an understatement. No amount of description equals the information contained in one photograph. So, the *entire* book revolves around the presentation of the picture. The design of every page in the body of this book is, therefore, based on the clearest, most spectacular presentation of the specimens possible.

For this book to serve as an effective and powerful reference tool for buyers, resellers and enthusiasts, every photo on every page in this book meets certain standards. First, for any given fish, both the male and the female are *always* shown. It is never one or the other. Only one type of cichlid appears per page. The fish pictured are always prime, adult specimens in good natural color. No hormones are used.

Simplicity is a definite prerequisite for clarity. Therefore, all basic information is presented either as icons or brief, clearly placed text. Everything on the page is available to you in one glance.

Simplicity also plays a part in the organization of the book. Every fish is listed under a *variety* of names commonly in use among hobbyists and professionals. Each listing leads directly to a specific page, eliminating the need to search from listing-to-listing in the index to find what you need. Any cichlid in this book should be able to be located within seconds.

This emphasis on simplicity and clarity stems from one very important fact about this book: *it is written from a commercial—not academic—standpoint*. In other words, we have not padded the book with unnecessary text. The goal when writing this book was to be concise and accurate. That means little text, all written from a practical, commercial standpoint. Also, all the information presented is a result of years of personal experience in commercial breeding. There is no second-hand information.

There is an old saying: "too many cooks spoil the soup." Well, there are already enough cooks in the academic kitchen adding their own ingredients to the cichlid industry's soup of names, classifications and scholarly speculation. We are *not* ichthyologists. We are not aiming to classify fish. We are not aiming to favor one commonly used name over another. Let the scientists and academics wrangle over the proper classifications. We only care about the names—common or scientific—that people *currently* use. A good example of this is *Red Top Aristochromis. Red Top Aristochromis* does not properly belong in the *Aristochromis* family. However, this name is commonly used and widely recognized. Therefore, it is among the names we included the fish under in both the index and on the page.

We hope this text proves enjoyable and useful for you. We are confident that you will find this a powerful reference, filled with spectacular photography. Assuming this book does well, we plan to publish future volumes. Each volume will be a distinct product, containing an entirely new set of fish. While this first volume mainly features Malawi Cichlids, future volumes will deal heavily with other cichlids (including cichlids from Lake Tanganyika, Lake Victoria and South America).

VORWORT

Die grundlegenden Ziele, dieses Buch herauszugeben, können in 3 Worten umrissen werden: *Klarheit, Klarheit* und *Klarheit.* Leider ist das ein rarer Begriff, wenn man mit Cichliden zu tun hat. Die meisten Berufszweige besitzen eine gemeinsame Basis von Namen und Bezeichnungen, aufgrund derer miteinander verhandelt wird, ohne seine Zuflucht zu Gesten und Umschreibungen nehmen zu müssen.

Unglücklicherweise ist diese Basis in der Welt der Cichliden zumindest schwankend. Seit den frühen 70er Jahren, als afrikanische Cichliden für Händler und Liebhaber in größerem Maßstabe erhältlich wurden, sind in erstaunlichen Mengen neue Arten und Farbvarianten entdeckt und dem Konsumenten ver-fügbar gemacht worden. Diese Flut hat es den Wissenschaftlern unmöglich gemacht, mit der Klassifizierung und Beschreibung der Fische Schritt zu halten. Das Ergebnis ist ein sprachlicher Turmbau zu Babel, bestehend aus einem Wirrwarr unterschiedlicher und unbeständiger Händlernamen.

Dieses Fehlen einen definitiven Taxonomie hat ein Vakuum erzeugt, in dem ein wilder Dschungel aus verschiedenen Händlernamen und interessanten Kombinationen aus Händler – und wissenschaftlichen Namen wuchert, meistens basierend auf Klassifizierungen, die aufs Geratewohl erstellt wurden.

Es gibt zwei grundlegende Erscheinungen in diesem speziellen Namenssystem: das *viele Fische für einen Namen* und das *viele Namen für einen Fisch* – Syndrom.

Ein wunderschönes Beispiel für die erste Situation, viele Fische für einen Namen, ist *Aulonocara Stuartgranti.* Dieser Name wurde gleich *drei* äußerlich unterschiedlichen Fischen gegeben, dem *Yellowsided – Ngara* – und dem *Flavescens* Kaiser buntbarsch. Solche Situationen erschweren noch zusätzlich die Aufgabe, diese Fische klar und präzise aufzulisten und zu behandeln.

Das zweite Syndrom—einem Fisch viele Namen zu geben—taucht bei fast jedem Cichliden auf. Selten findet sich ein Exemplar, das nicht verschiedene Namen besitzt. Oft sind das ein "wissenschaftlicher" Name, mehrere Händlernamen sowie einige Kombinationen von beidem.

Cichliden–Namen sind immer wieder Gegenstand von Klassifizierungs – Änderungen. Deshalb tendiert jeder Autor eines Cichlidenbuches dazu, sein favorisiertes Namenssystem aufzugreifen und andere auszuschließen. Das führt natürlich dazu, daß nicht kundige Leser nur schwer finden, was sie suchen.

Ein gutes Beispiel dafür war die Klassifizierung einer Vielzahl von Fischen in die Gattung *Haplochromis,* der Vereinfachung zuliebe. Doch sobald das fest etabliert war, erfolgte eine erneute Aufspaltung in die alten Gattungs—Klassifizierungen *Dimidiochromis, Copadichromis, Sciaenochromis* etc.

Diese Inkonsequenz, gepaart mit regionalen Unterschieden (zum Beispiel die zwischen Europa und den USA), weicht die gemeinsame Basis noch weiter auf, von dem wir für eine klare, verläßliche Kommunikation innerhalb der Cichliden-Welt abhängen.

Alle diese Probleme führen uns fast zwangsläufig zurück zu dem Zweck dieses Buches. Klarheit. Die Philosophie hinter diesem Werk beruht auf dem dringenden Bedarf eines photographischen Nachschlagewerks für Cichliden, welches das Hauptaugenmerk auf eine klare, präzise Präsentation legt.

Ein Bild sagt mehr als tausend Worte, sagt ein altes geflügeltes Wort. Das ist eine Untertreibung. *Keine* Beschreibung enthält soviel Information wie ein Foto. Deswegen dreht sich das gesamte Buch fast ausschließlich um die Präsentation von Bildern. Die Anlage jeder Seite dieses Bandes basiert auf der klarstmöglichen, schönsten Präsentation eines Fisches.

Damit dieses Buch als effektives und aussagekräftiges Referenzmittel für Käufer, Verkäufer und Enthusiasten dienen kann, wurden an jedes Foto auf jeder Seite bestimmte Maßstäbe angelegt. Als erstes werden *immer* von jedem dargestellten Fisch sowohl Männchen als auch Weibchen gezeigt. Es ist nie nur einer von beiden. Die abgebildeten Fische sind immer erstklassige adulte Tiere in guter natürlicher Farbe. Es wurden keine Hormone benutzt.

Einfachheit ist eine wichtige Voraussetzung für Klarheit. Deswegen sind alle Grundinformationen entweder als Symbole oder kurzer, präziser Text dargestellt. Alles auf einer Seite ist auf einen Blick ersichtlich.

Einfachheit spielt auch bei der Organisation des Buches eine Rolle. Jeder Fische ist unter einer Anzahl verschiedener Namen aufgelistet, die gewöhnlich unter Hobbyisten und Professionellen benutzt werden. Jeder Name führt direkt zu einer Seitenzahl, um eine Suche von Name zu Name im Index zu vermeiden. Jeder Cichlide in diesem Buch sollte in Sekunden zu finden sein.

Diese Betonung auf Einfachheit und Klarheit rührt von einer sehrwichtigen Tatsache über dieses Buch her: *Es ist von einem kommerziellen—nicht wissenschaftlichen—Standpunkt aus geschrieben.* Mit anderen Worten, wir haben das Buch nicht mit unnötigem Text versehen. Das Ziel war es, kurz und prägnant zu sein. Das bedeutet wenig Text, alles aus praktischer, kommerzieller Sicht geschrieben. Außerdem ist alle dargestellte Information das Resultat langjähriger persönlicher Erfahrungen.

Ein altes Sprichwort sagt: "Viele Köche verderben den Brei". Es gibt schon genug Köche in der akademischen Küche, die ihre eigenen Zutaten zum Brei der Cichliden–Welt aus Namen, Klassifizierungen und wissenschaftlichen Spekulationen hinzufügen. Wir sind *keine* Ichthyologen. Wir sind nicht darauf aus, Fische zu klassifizieren. Wir wollen nicht einen gebräuchlichen Namen dem anderen vorziehen. Wir überlassen es Wissenschaftlern und Akademikern, sich über ordentliche Klassifizierungen zu streiten. Wir interessieren uns nur für die gegenwärtig im Umlauf befindlichen Namen. Ein gutes Beispiel dafür ist *Red Top Aristochromis. Red Top Aristochromis* gehört wahrscheinlich nicht zur Gattung *Aristochromis.* Trotzdem ist dieser Name gebräuchlich und weltweit bekannt. Deshalb schlossen wir diesen Namen sowohl auf der betreffenden Seite als auch in den Index mit ein.

Wir hoffen, bewiesen zu haben: dieses Buch ist sowohl schön anzusehen als auch nützlich für Sie. Wir sind sicher, Sie werden eine aussagekräftige Referenzmöglichkeit, gespickt mit spektakulären Fotos, finden. In der Annahme, daß dieses Buch den Gefallen der Käufer findet, planen wir die Herausgabe weiterer Bände. Jedes Buch soll ein präzises Werk mit einem ganz anderen Sortiment an Fischarten und - Varianten werden. Während der vorliegende Band hauptsächlich Malawi-Cichliden behandelt, werden sich zukünftige Bände ausführlich mit anderen Cichliden beschäftigen (einschließlich Tanganjikasee, Viktoriasee und Südamerika).

前言

本書最主要的目的是：清楚、簡單、實用。

自七十年代以來，由非洲輸入美國或歐洲的鳳凰魚，不但進口快速而且種類繁多，以致科學家沒有時間仔細調查分類，給以適當學名，造成許多種魚共用一個名字，或一種魚擁有幾個名字的現象，於是，不必說也可以想像到的結果是—矛盾、混亂。

俗語說：「百聞不如一見」，這就是本書所依據的原則：書中所有的魚都以準確的天然彩色照片來舉例說明。同時，本書的寫作是根據商業的觀點而非科學家的觀點，因此，關於魚的類別及其標準學名，還是留待科學家去討論吧！

書中所發表的意見均來自二十五年在養魚場的實際經驗，並非一般書本上的知識。

若要查詢魚名，請按英文字母順序查詢，無論用學名或俗稱均可查得正確頁數，因為本書將魚的名稱不論是拉丁文或英文俗稱都放在索引內。

本書是叢書出版的第一冊，其中大半魚種來自馬拉維湖。在未來出版的書中，將會加入更多慈鯛科，包括來自担加尼加湖、維多利亞湖、中南美洲和西非洲等地。

深信本書在國際慈鯛科貿易上會有很大、很實際的貢獻。

USER'S GUIDE

I. THE ORGANIZATION OF THE BOOK

This book was organized with an eye toward simplicity. Every cichlid in this guide was listed, *alphabetically*, by its primary name. There are no subdivisions or other criteria to complicate this straightforward arrangement. It is important to note that the choices for the primary names were based on the need for *simplicity.* The selection does not reflect any belief that one name is more valid than another. We're not here to pass judgement.

II. FINDING WHAT YOU NEED

If you look at a page in this book, you'll notice that—in addition to the *primary* name listed in red—*secondary* names are displayed as well. These synonyms are each listed *individually* in the scientific and/or trade index. Therefore, you can locate any fish in this book via looking up one of a variety of commonly used names. If a name is common, it is included *even if the name is not scientifically correct.* In addition, each name in the index leads directly to a page in this guide, eliminating the need for tedious cross-referencing. And—since each variety is given exactly one page —each entry lists only one page for each fish.

III. THE MALE AND FEMALE

For the sake of clarity, every page in this book is arranged identically. The male of each specimen is *always* the top picture. Likewise, the female is *always* the bottom picture. Other elements which are standard on every page, the ***size icon*** and the ***region,*** are described below.

IV. THE SIZE ICONS

Instead of burying the size information in the text, we use ***size icons***—located in the upper corner of every page. These icons provide simple, at-a-glance information about the size of the fish. There are three (3) symbols, each of which represent either ***small***, ***medium*** or ***large***. The size ranges that makeup each category are listed below.

Small
Less than 9cm.
(3.5 in.)

Medium
9 cm. – 15cm.
(3.5 in. – 6 in.)

Large
More than 15cm.
(6 in.)

V. THE NATIVE REGION

The region from which each fish originates is listed directly under the size icons. This allows you to take in all the basic information about that cichlid at-a-glance.

COLOFON

The layout and design of this book was created by **Ian M. Tepoot** using *Aldus PageMaker 5.0 for Windows* on a generic Intel-based 486/66 DX2 computer. The initial text was written using *Word Perfect 5.2 for Windows.*

The size icons and New Life Publishing logo was created in *Adobe Illustrator Version 4 for Windows* by I. Tepoot.

Typesetting was likewise performed in PageMaker 5.0 for Windows. Typefaces used in the creation of this book are: *Adobe Gill Sans, Adobe Optima* and *Adobe Industria In-line* for the cover. Chinese characters for the cover were produced with *Adobe Illustrator Version 4 for Windows.*

Finally, the images were scanned and processed using a *Linotype-Hell S3800 Scanner and a Silicon Graphics Indigo II workstation.*

ARISTOCHROMIS CHRISTYI

There are two factors that make *A. christyi* a rather unique fish. First, *A. christyi* is currently the only cichlid in the *Aristochromis* genus. Second, *A. christyi* is of the few fish whose mating season is early March. On a practical level, it is important to note that—while not a generally aggressive fish—*A. christyi* will consume any fish small enough for it to swallow easily.

ASTATOTILAPIA BICOLOR
Piebold Redfin

The *A. bicolor* pair shown here are OB morphs. The standard male is black with red edging on its fins. *A. bicolor* produces male and female OB morphs on a regular basis. The OB variation of this cichlid has an advantage over the standard form. The standard male, like most Victorian Cichlids, loses its color when under stress. On the other hand, the *A. bicolor* OB morph maintains its color under all conditions.

ASTATOTILAPIA KAYENZI
Haplochromis kayenzi

A. kayenzi sports a vivid red patch along its flank. However, as with most Victorian Cichlids, *A. kayenzi* has one disadvantage. Under stress, this cichlid will lose a majority of its color.

LAKE VICTORIA

ASTATOTILAPIA OBLIQUIDENS

Haplochromis obliquidens

A. obliquidens is among the more attractive of the Victorian Cichlids. Red is the most common color in ornamental Victorian Cichlids. Therefore, *A. obliquidens'* yellow and aquamarine color scheme—combined with its striping—give this fish a fairly unique appearance. Another advantage of this fish is that it fades less than most Victorian Cichlids when under stress.

ASTATOTILAPIA OBLIQUIDENS (ZEBRA)
Haplochromis obliquidens (Zebra)
Zebra Obliquidens

This *A. obliquidens* variety stands out among Victorian Cichlids because of its thick vertical stripes. This feature is, of course, why this fish was dubbed "*zebra*". *A. obliquidens (Zebra)* also differs from other Victorians because it does not fade as easily. The stripes remain visible under most conditions.

ASTATOTILAPIA RUBRIPINNIS
Velvet Blue Scraper

As of 1994, *A. rubripinnis* is the newest import from Lake Victoria. The female shown here is an OB morph. This is interesting because OB morphs are quite rare among Victorian Cichlids.

ASTATOTILAPIA RUBROCORPUS
Cherry Red Astatotilapia

A. rubrocorpus is one of the most attractive of the Victorian Cichlids. Red is the most common color among Victorians. However, *A. rubrocorpus*' delicate red front that fades into green toward the rear creates an extremely complimentary color scheme. One advantage that *A. rubrocorpus* shares with most Victorian Cichlids is a prolific nature. Victorians begin breeding when young, breed often and enjoy large spawns.

ASTATOTILAPIA SPINOSIGNIS
Flame Back

Prior to the 1980's, when people mentioned Victorian Cichlids, the immediate reaction was *bland*. *A. spinosignis* was one of the first truly spectacular cichlids to be exported from Lake Victoria. However, through random, careless breeding the red color adorning this cichlid's back began to fade. The specimen shown here is the result of *reversing* that process. Through selective breeding, this fish's color has regained its former intensity.

AULONOCARA BAENSCHI
Aulonocara benga
Sunshine Peacock

There are at least two varieties of *A. baenschi,* originating in different areas of the lake. The specimen depicted here is particularly attractive, sporting a rich lemon yellow body and blue face. In contrast, the other—often referred to as *Aulonocara maleri*—lacks this blue color on the face.

AULONOCARA CAROLINAE

Aulonocara carolae
Trematocranus carolinae
Swallowtail Peacock

The main feature of *A. carolinae* is its large swallowtail. This is a unique feature. Of all the Malawi Cichlids presently known, this fish's tail is the largest relative to its body. Although *A. carolinae*'s tail is impressive, I believe that selective breeding can enhance this trait further. Such carefully controlled breeding could take this cichlid from attractive to spectacular.

AULONOCARA CONTRATUS
Redeye Flavescens Peacock

This mutation from Belgium has extremely strange coloration. Despite its albino-like red eyes, this cichlid contains blue and black, which is generally absent in albino fish. This makes *A. contratus* the only presently known fish with this set of traits. Hence the name *contratus*—or *contradiction*—peacock.

LAKE MALAWI

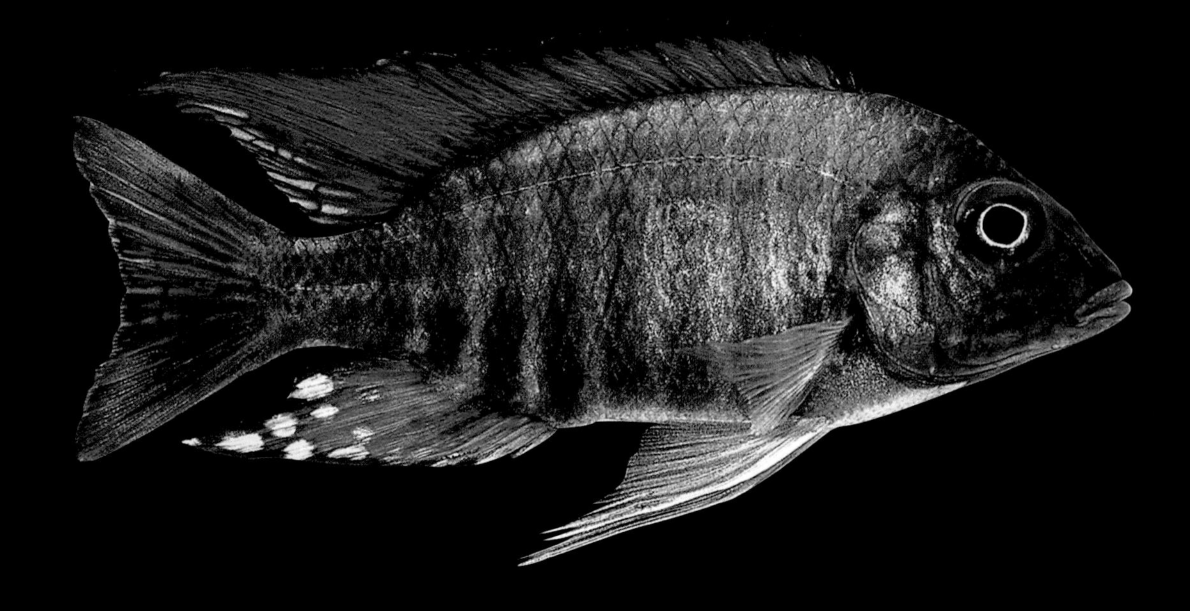

AULONOCARA ETHELWYNNAE
Aulonocara chitande
Chitande Peacock

A. ethelwynnae is a very dark fish with iridescent fins. Like all *Aulonocara*, this fish tends to maintain its color throughout the year. This is a desirable selling trait of *A. ethelwynnae* and—in fact—all peacocks.

AULONOCARA FLAVESCENS
Aulonocara usisya
Flavescens Peacock

This fish has maintained a steadily high market value despite being available since the early 1970's. This economic longevity can be attributed to the vigorous demand and the consistently limited number being produced.

AULONOCARA FLAVESCENS (BLUE DORSAL)
Blue Dorsal Flavescens Peacock
Blue Neon Peacock

Like most peacocks, to the untrained eye, the female and juveniles of *A. flavescens (Blue Dorsal)* look virtually identical to the female and young of almost every other peacock. Breeders beware! Situations like these are ripe for unintentional hybridizing. One way to combat this is to administer testosterone to the females. This will cause the distinct male coloration to become evident, allowing the breeder to properly identify and pair the male and female fish.

AULONOCARA FREIBERGI
Trematocranus freibergi
Butterfly Peacock

Fish which were previously classified in the genus *Trematocranus* (i.e. *A. regina* and *A. carolinae*) have *extremely* similar color schemes and markings. However, these cichlids are divided into two distinct variations: those whose overall coloring is light and those whose coloring is dark. Also, all *Trematocranus* have a common problem. They tend to develop cataracts.

AULONOCARA KANDEENSIS
Blue Orchid Peacock
Kande Island Peacock

This fish is among the smallest of the peacocks. Luckily, its spawns are quite numerous due to the extremely small size of the eggs. Also, while *A. kandeensis* closely resembles *Aulonocara maylandi*, *A. maylandi* is prone to losing its color. *A. kandeensis* has more stable coloration.

AULONOCARA LWANDA
Lwanda Peacock

Like many fish pictured in this book, *A. lwanda* is a new import as of 1994. Generally, it takes approximately 4 to 5 years after a cichlid is first imported for it to become readily available. Interestingly, *A. lwanda* imports seem to consist of more than one geographic race. Each has slight variations on the general *lwanda* color scheme. The specimen shown here is, in my opinion, one of the more lovely varieties.

AULONOCARA MAMELELA
Mamelela Peacock
Mandarina Peacock

First imported in 1992, *A. mamelela* is a spectacular fish. There seem to be two color varieties from the lake: mandarin orange and yellow. Variations such as this can provide the savvy breeder with an opportunity to "custom tailor" the appearance of all subsequent generations. He or she can help determine the future of this fish. The *A. mamelela* shown here belongs to the mandarin orange variety.

AULONOCARA MAULANA
Maulana Peacock

This peacock was first imported in 1994. The spectacular velvet blue on *A. maulana's* face and bright yellow markings behind the gills virtually ensures its popularity in years to come.

LAKE MALAWI

AULONOCARA MBENJI
Aulonocara stuartgranti
Yellowsided Peacock

First introduced in the 1970's, *A. mbenji* is an old standby which has maintained its market value over the years. This peacock looks similar to *A. ngara*. In fact, *A. mbenji* and *A. ngara* may be different color varieties of the same species from various areas of the lake.

AULONOCARA MBENJI (ALBINO)
Aulonocara stuartgranti (Albino)
Albino Yellowsided Peacock

The albino form of *A. mbenji*, developed in the U.S., was the *first* albino peacock ever produced. Understandably, the *A. mbenji (Albino)* gained immediate and lasting popularity, particularly in the Orient.

AULONOCARA MOZAMBIQUE
Regal Peacock

This peacock is relatively small, with a bright metallic blue color. Like most peacocks, this fish is quite docile. This is a desirable selling trait of *A. mozambique* and—in fact—all peacocks.

AULONOCARA NGARA
Ngara Peacock

This fish is among the most striking of the peacocks. The distinct fluorescent blue and intense orange areas give this fish a sharp two-toned appearance.

AULONOCARA NIGRIPINNIS
Orange Collar Peacock

Though not the most colorful peacock, *A. nigripinnis* is still an interesting fish. It possesses black fins, which are an unusual trait. Also, *A. nigripinnis*, most likely, has a solid commercial future. Almost all members of the *Aulonocara* genus are good sellers.

AULONOCARA NYASSAE
Aulonocara hansbaenschi
Red Flush Peacock
Redsided Peacock

The particular specimen pictured here is the result of selective breeding. Its tail is significantly larger than that of the standard *A. nyassae*. Also, the red area on this fish is more abundant and intensely colored than is generally seen. This specimen is a compelling argument for a controlled, selective breeding program.

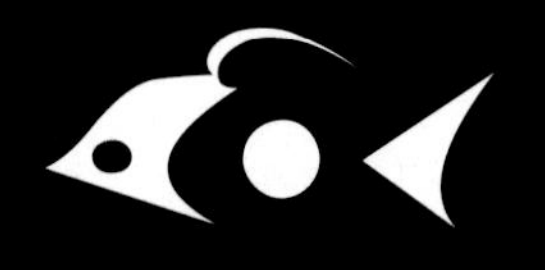

AULONOCARA NYASSAE (MUTATION)
Squirrel Peacock

This is another odd mutation from Belgium (the other is *A. contratus*). *A. nyassae (Mutation)* is the only presently known *brown* peacock. The brown color—combined with the odd, large-pupiled eyes resembling that of a squirrel—has earned this fish the name "*Squirrel Peacock*". This cichlid is living proof that color mutations are more frequent (and more radical) than is commonly known. The wise breeder will be quick to *capitalize* on such opportunities.

AULONOCARA REGINA
Trematocranus eureka
Trematocranus regina
Red Trematocranus Freibergi

Credit where credit is due. **The European developers of *A. regina* have created a magnificent fish. This variety does not occur *at all* in the wild. It is a good example of an engineered fish that has been accepted because of its beauty. Furthermore, I believe that continued development of *A. regina* could enhance this fish's bright orange/red color even more.**

AULONOCARA ROBERTI
Aulonocara korneliae
Orange Shoulder Peacock

The female peacocks of all varieties look virtually identical to the untrained eye. *A. roberti* is no exception. A situation such as this is fertile ground for unintentional hybrids. Such random crossings often degenerate the beauty and uniqueness of the fish. Breeders should go through the effort of properly pairing the fish. Simple tests (such as the hormone method described on page 14) and a bit more vigilance can prevent such hybrids.

AULONOCARA ROSTRATUM

Longnose Peacock

This peacock's long nose and large size give *A. rostratum* a distinct appearance. In fact, this is the largest presently known variety of peacock. *A. rostratum*'s color does not maintain its intensity all year round. However, its color increases greatly during the mating season.

AULONOCARA RUBESCENS
Red Peacock

Bravo to the developer of *A. rubescens.* This is among the most spectacular of the peacocks. This fish, which does not occur at all in the wild, was developed in Europe. *A. rubescens* is a fantastic example of an engineered, man-made fish that is accepted because of its exceptional beauty. In addition, I am sure this beauty was an *intentionally* developed trait, given by a careful, vigilant breeder.

AULONOCARA SAULOSI
Green Face Peacock

This peacock is distinctive in two ways. First, it's the only peacock with blue/green coloration on its face. Second, its anal fin has an exceptionally large number of egg spots. This old import's popularity has suffered because of limited availability.

CHAMPSOCHROMIS CAERULEUS
Trout Cichlid

C. caeruleus elongated, torpedo shape and extended fins make this an extremely attractive cichlid. However, this fish is quite aggressive with its own kind during mating season. Also, *C. caeruleus* will eat any fish small enough for it to readily swallow. So be careful mixing this fish with other, smaller fish.

CHAMPSOCHROMIS SPILORHYNCHUS

The appearance of this cichlid is very similar to that of *C. caeruleus.* The only obvious physical dissimilarities are the deeper body and a pronounced black teardrop marking in front of the eyes.

CHILOTILAPIA EUCHILUS

The wild *C. euchilus* has a large, fleshy lip. However, by the first domestically-bred generation this trait disappears. This serves as an easy way to distinguish the wild and domestic fish from one another.

CHILOTILAPIA RHOADESII

This fish has the deepest body of any presently known Malawi Cichlid. This trait, in addition to its bright metallic-blue color, makes this a desirable fish. The extreme depth of its body gives this cichlid a deceptively stubby appearance. Also, the female *C. rhoadesii* is highly colorful.

CYATHOPHARYNX FURCIFER (GREEN NEON)
Green Neon

In my opinion, this is the most attractive of the genus *Cyathopharynx*. This is due to its iridescent scales and multicolored finnage. In addition, the colors intensify even further during mating, making *C. furcifer (Green Neon)* truly a sight to behold.

CYNOTILAPIA AFRA (CHIMATE)
Dwarf Afra

C. afra (Chimate) **is the smallest member of the *Cynotilapia* genus. Hence the name *Dwarf Afra*. This fish is both extremely attractive and peaceful. It is, in fact, the *most* docile of all the *afras*. However, this cichlid has not yet firmly established a domestic strain. Therefore, availability is limited.**

CYNOTILAPIA AFRA (CLOWN)
Clown Afra

The female specimen pictured here is a mutation variety. Generally, the female is a grey color. The male shown is a standard male. However, this mutation—which is not a hybrid—can produce both standard and OB variations of the male and female. This is a perfect example of taking a fortunate mutation and *capitalizing* on it, rather than allowing a desirable trait to disappear back into the gene pool through carelessness.

CYNOTILAPIA AFRA (LION COVE)
Lion Cove Afra

The *Lion Cove Afra* is beautiful, but highly aggressive toward its own kind. If you put two or more males of this variety together in a small tank with no hiding places, the result is predictable. The dominant male will kill the other males in the tank. Because of this, the market for this attractive fish is somewhat lukewarm.

CYNOTILAPIA AFRA (MBAMBA)
Mbamba Afra

This cichlid is very similar in appearance to the *Red Top Afra*. The only obvious visual difference is its darker coloration and white blaze on the forehead area.

CYNOTILAPIA AFRA (RED TOP)
Red Top Afra

This cichlid is among the earliest imports in the *C. afra* species. However, the domestic strain has never been readily available in quantity.

CYNOTILAPIA AFRA (SULFURHEAD)
Sulfurhead Afra

C. afra (Sulfurhead) is, overall, the best of the *afras*. It is less aggressive than most *afra* varieties, as well as the most attractive. Like all Malawi Cichlids, this fish is a mouth brooder. This means that the fish will incubate its eggs in her mouth. The mother spits the fry out when they are free-swimming.

CYPHOTILAPIA FRONTOSA (ZAIRE BLUE)

As of 1994, the *Zaire Blue* variety of *C. frontosa* is the newest and most expensive of the *frontosa* varieties. It is also, in my opinion, the most spectacular member of this species.

CYPHOTILAPIA FRONTOSA (ZAMBIA)

Like all *C. frontosa*, the Zambian variety is among the most popular cichlids in the industry. This is particularly true in the Orient. The *Zambia* variety is somewhat less common than other, previously imported *C. frontosa* varieties. As of 1994, one notable exception is *C. frontosa (Zaire Blue)*.

CYPRICHROMIS SPECIES (NEON)

As of 1994, *C. species (Neon)* is a new import. I do not believe that this fish will ever become a staple in the cichlid industry. *C. species (Neon)* produces few young—as little as 10 per spawn. Also, these few fry are very hard to collect from the mouth, due to this cichlid's exceptionally small mouth.

TANGANYIKA

CYPRICHROMIS UTINTA

C. utinta is a very atypical-looking cichlid. In my opinion, this fish does not even resemble a cichlid. *C. utinta* is one of the more colorful of the *Cyprichromis* genus. In addition, the adults can thrive on a diet of baby brine shrimp.

GNATHOCHROMIS PERMAXILLIARIS

This is a exceedingly odd-looking deep water fish. These bizarre looks may be attributed to its large eyes, long pelvic fins and duck-like plate lip. *G. permaxilliaris* is rather rare, suggesting a continued high price.

HAPLOCHROMIS AHLI
Sciaenochromis ahli
Electric Blue

A perennial favorite, *H. ahli* is perhaps the most spectacular cichlid today. Its color can rival that of salt water fish. This cichlid has enjoyed a consistently high market value for over 20 years, due to its beauty and peaceful nature. Unfortunately, *H. ahli* is prone to Hexamita parasites.

HAPLOCHROMIS BILINEATUS
Turquoise Haplochromis

Rare among hobbyists, *H. bilineatus* is probably fairly common in the wild. This obscurity may be attributed to the fact that its picture has never been published, revealing its rich turquoise color.

HAPLOCHROMIS BORLEYI (EASTERN)
Copadichromis verduyni
Eastern Borleyi

H. borleyi (Eastern) looks similar to *H. quadrimaculatus* except that it is a smaller fish, possessing more blue coloration. This cichlid is very peaceful. In fact—if the tank is large enough, with plenty of hiding places—the fry can remain with the adults. They won't actively hunt the young.

HAPLOCHROMIS BORLEYI (GOLD FIN)
Copadichromis borleyi (Gold Fin)
Gold Fin Borleyi

This is among the most beautiful of the *H. borleyi*. Its long pelvic fins make for a striking appearance. Despite its beauty, this cichlid is relatively inexpensive. This is because *Gold Fin Borleyi* is an exceedingly prolific fish. The result, understandably, is that the *Gold Fin Borleyi* is quite common.

HAPLOCHROMIS BORLEYI (KADANGO)
Copadichromis borleyi (Kadango)
Kadango Borleyi
Red Fin Borleyi

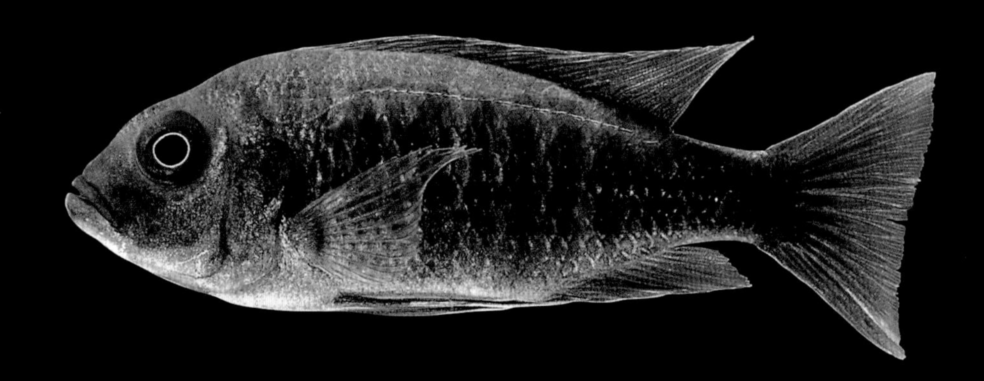

The *Red Fin Borleyi* used to be quite expensive. However, the price has dropped significantly recently. In our opinion, this fish is less attractive than the *Gold Fin Borleyi*, the *Red Fin Borleyi*'s pelvic fins are shorter than those of the *Gold Fin* variety.

HAPLOCHROMIS CHRYSOGASTER
Otopharynx chrysogaster

H. chrysogaster is—I believe—destined to be a very popular cichlid. This is a beautiful fish sporting a creamy, pastel yellow color. As of today, *H. chrysogaster* is not readily available in the United States. It's what might be called a "hidden treasure." This fish's true appearance is known to very few.

HAPLOCHROMIS CHRYSONOTUS (AZUREUS)
Copadichromis azureus
Electric Blue II

H. chrysonotus (Azureus) was first introduced in the U.S. as *H. ovatus*. It was later named both *H. chrysonotus* and *Copadichromis azureus*. This is a perfect illustration of the confusing name game being played in the cichlid world. The specimen shown here has exceptionally long pelvic fins. If a breeder judges this to be an improvement, he or she *should* use such mutations as a foundation for his or her breeding stock.

HAPLOCHROMIS CHRYSONOTUS (CHRYSONOTUS)
Copadichromis chrysonotus

H. chrysonotus (Chrysonotus) is what might be called the *true chrysonotus*. However, the cichlid which is *now* called *Copadichromis azureus* had been known as *H. chrysonotus* for so long that the name had become thoroughly entrenched. This is where our "unscientific" classification comes in handy. To identify this "true" *chrysonotus*, we simply named it *H. chrysonotus (Chrysonotus)* to distinguish it from what is now called either *H. chrysonotus (Azureus)* or *C. azureus*.

HAPLOCHROMIS CHRYSONOTUS (ICEBERG)
Copadichromis azureus (Iceberg)
Iceberg Chrysonotus

C. chrysonotus (Iceberg) **is one of the most praiseworthy fish in this book. It is peaceful and extremely attractive. One look at the photo tells the whole story. This fish is stunning. I believe that this cichlid (which is a fairly new import) is destined for greatness.**

HAPLOCHROMIS COMPRESSICEPS

Dimidiochromis compressiceps

A great injustice has been done to *H. compressiceps*. Contrary to some previously published myths, this cichlid *does not eat the eyeballs of other fish*. Therefore, the label "Malawi Eye Biter" is totally inappropriate. In fact, a better name for *H. compressiceps* would be the "Playboy of Malawi". This fish will try to mate with virtually any other Malawi Cichlid.

LAKE MALAWI

HAPLOCHROMIS COMPRESSICEPS (ALBINO)
Dimidiochromis compressiceps (Albino)
Albino Compressiceps

This is perhaps the *first* albino *Haplochromis* produced in the U.S. Because of its elegant shape, the regular form of *H. compressiceps* is a good seller. Combine this trait with an albino's commercial potential, and you have a fish which is *sure* to take-off like a rocket in the cichlid industry. As of 1994, *albino compressiceps* is not established in the cichlid market.

HAPLOCHROMIS CYANEUS

Copadichromis cyaneus

Though a peaceful and colorful fish, *H. cyaneus*' commercial potential is questionable. This is because *H. cyaneus*' color scheme is very similar to that of *H. borleyi*-type cichlids. There are already so many fish with this color scheme that—though attractive—the future demand for this cichlid is doubtful.

LAKE MALAWI

HAPLOCHROMIS ELECTRA
Placidochromis electra
Deep Water Haplochromis

H. electra **is exceptionally peaceful. This, combined with *H. electra*'s delicate, pastel blue coloring has given this fish popularity that has endured since the 1970's. Given a large enough tank with many hiding places, this fish's fry does *not* have to be removed from the parents' tank. The adults won't actively hunt the young.**

HAPLOCHROMIS ELECTRA (NOVA)
Placidochromis electra (Nova)
Super Blue Electra

H. electra (Nova), first introduced in 1993, has an appearance similar to *H. electra* except for its bright, electric blue/purple coloring. The juveniles of this fish—sporting a black and white dorsal—are particularly attractive compared to many *Haplochromis* young.

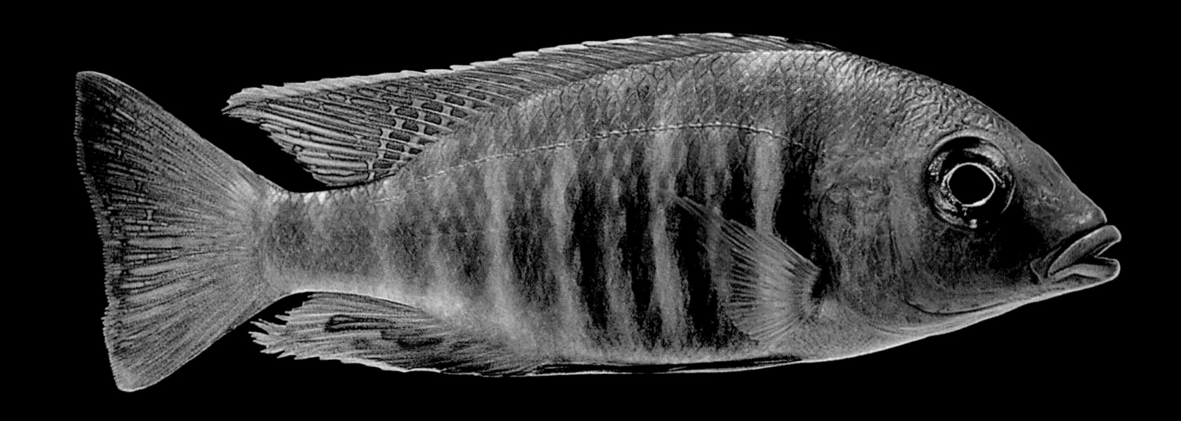

HAPLOCHROMIS ELECTRA (YELLOW)
Placidochromis electra (Yellow)
Yellow Deep Water Haplochromis

H. electra (Yellow) may be an *H. electra* color variation from a different part of the lake. It looks very much like *H. electra* except for an abundance of yellow on its underbelly and fins. As of 1994, this fish is a new import. Its commercial potential is good, due to its beauty and docile nature.

HAPLOCHROMIS FENESTRATUS (MAGUNGA)
Protomelas fenestratus (Magunga)

Like all *fenestratus* varieties, *H. fenestratus (Magunga)* is both colorful and *exceptionally* peaceful. This peacefulness can be demonstrated by the fact that this cichlid's young can remain safely in a large pond with the *H. fenestratus* adults.

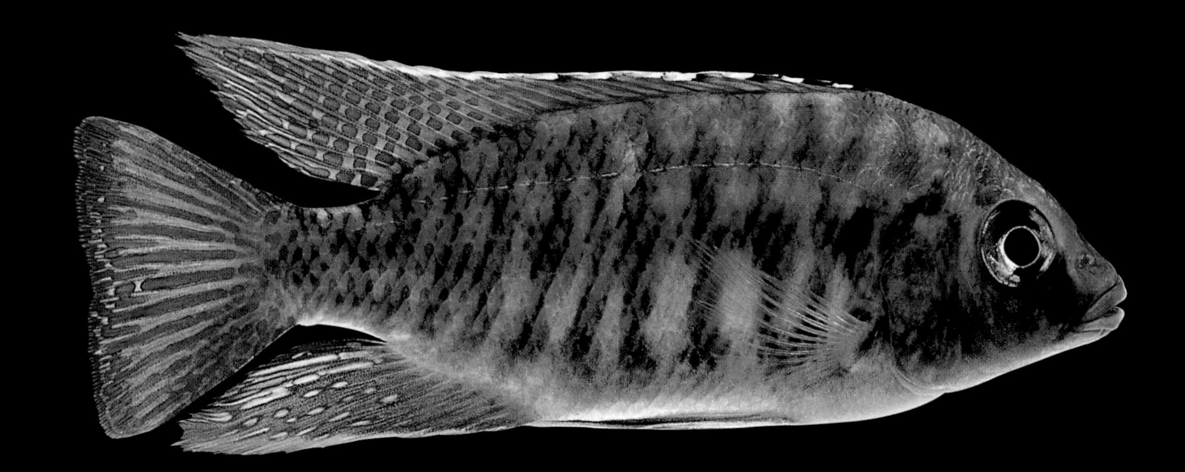

HAPLOCHROMIS FENESTRATUS (MKALI)
Protomelas fenestratus (Mkali)
Blue & Gold Fenestratus

H. fenestratus (Mkali) looks extremely similar to *H. fenestratus (Magunga)* except for a bright gold underbelly. This is why the fish is called *Blue & Gold Fenestratus*. I personally prefer the *Mkali* variety over the *Magunga* variety because of the *Blue & Gold Fenestratus'* two-toned appearance.

HAPLOCHROMIS FENESTRATUS (TAIWAN REEF)

Protomelas fenestratus (Taiwan Reef)
Taiwan Reef Fenestratus

Like all members of the *fenestratus* species, *H. fenestratus (Taiwan Reef)* does not actively prey on other individuals' young. Also, the *Taiwan Reef* variety is extremely prolific. Because of this fish's small eggs, its spawns are quite large. As of 1994, *Taiwan Reef's* price is relatively high, since it is a new import. However, this fish's prolific nature will almost guarantee a future drop in price.

HAPLOCHROMIS FLAVIMANUS
Protomelas flavimanus

A very expensive fish in the 1970's, *H. flavimanus* has since dropped in price significantly. This cichlid has much to recommend it, including a peaceful nature and attractive coloring. Also, the wild *H. flavimanus* has a large, fleshy lip. However, by the first domestically-bred generation this trait disappears.

LAKE MALAWI

HAPLOCHROMIS FUSCOTAENIATUS
Nimbochromis fuscotaeniatus

This predator is aggressive toward other members of its species. It is, however, calm enough to be kept with other large cichlids. *H. fuscotaeniatus* has enjoyed unshaken popularity since the seventies. This can be largely attributed to its spectacular color and relatively attractive juveniles.

LAKE MALAWI

HAPLOCHROMIS HINDERI
Protomelas taeniolatus (Namalenje)
Red Empress

In the *Haplochromis* genus, burgundy red coloring is a rare and beautiful trait. So why—through careless and indiscriminate cross breeding—would anyone allow the *Red Empress*' most striking trait to be degraded? This is the *opposite* of what domestic breeding should do. Rather than degenerate a fish's natural appearance, a careful, selective breeding program should *enhance* a fish's beauty beyond that of its wild counterpart.

HAPLOCHROMIS HOLOTAENIA
Taeniochromis holotaenia

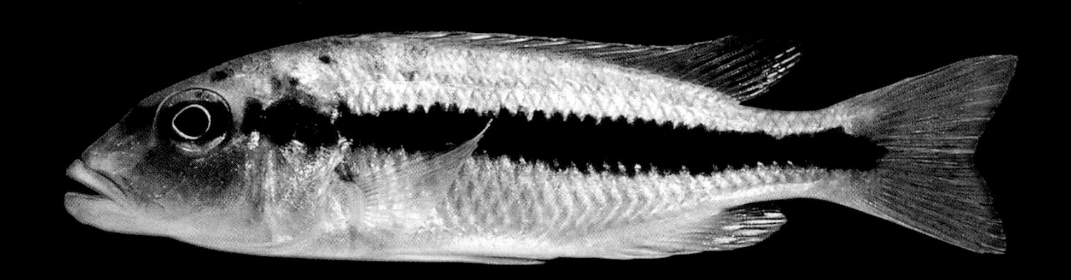

Because its picture has never been widely published and because of its present rarity in the United States, most people never see how spectacular this cichlid *really* is. This is yet another case of a "hidden treasure" in the cichlid world.

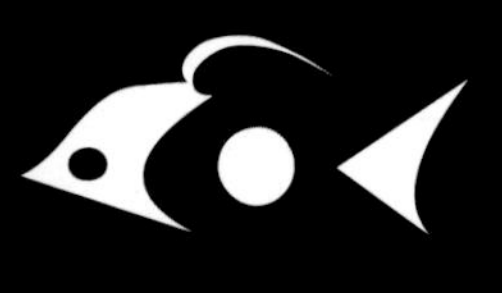

HAPLOCHROMIS INSIGNIS
Protomelas insignis

This fish resembles *H. fenestratus (Mkali)*. However, *H. insignis*' belly is a more intense gold than that of *H. fenestratus (Mkali)*. Also, the blue body of the *Blue & Gold Fenestratus* is replaced by a more green tinted blue on *H. insignis*' upper-half. This is yet another new fish from the lake. It was first imported in 1993.

HAPLOCHROMIS JACKSONI
Copadichromis jacksoni

Like all Rift Lake Cichlids, *H. jacksoni* thrives in hard alkaline water. pH values in the range between 7.6 and 8 are ideal. If your pH levels are *below* this, adding a substance called *Dolomite* to your tank will raise and maintain these ideal values. Another method is to add a little salt to the tank. Some companies even sell Rift Lake Salt for this purpose.

HAPLOCHROMIS JOHNSTONI

Placidochromis johnstoni

First imported during the 1970's as *Kachimangi*, *H. johnstoni* has one distinct trait. Namely, *H. johnstoni* has vertical bars on its body which are uncommonly wide. Predictably, there are less bars on its body than found in other cichlids with the thinner, common stripes.

HAPLOCHROMIS KIWINGE

Dimidiochromis kiwinge

H. kiwinge is one of the fastest moving Malawi Cichlids. Also, this cichlid is a predator. This *does not* mean, however, that it will be overly aggressive toward all other fish. Size is the only important factor. *H. kiwinge* will consume any fish small enough for it to swallow easily.

HAPLOCHROMIS LABRIDENS
Protomelas labridens

When this cichlid was first introduced, incorrectly identified as *H. strigatus*, it was mistakenly identified as a hybrid. This illustrates a common problem—namely a tendency among a few "experts" to render judgement before obtaining all the facts. In the future, such "experts" should be encouraged to keep an open mind and avoid rendering snap judgements.

HAPLOCHROMIS LEPTURUS (GREEN)
Buccochromis lepturus (Green)
Green Lepturus

If you have a large aquarium, the *Green Lepturus* is for you. This colorful fish can reach an impressive size. Its streamlined shape reveals its predatory nature. However, this should not be a problem. Simply avoid mixing this cichlid with other fish small enough for it to easily swallow.

HAPLOCHROMIS LEPTURUS (YELLOW)
Buccochromis rhoadesii
Yellow Lepturus

The *Yellow Lepturus* has two major advantages: impressive size and impressive coloration. Assuming you have a large enough tank, the *Yellow Lepturus* is a great addition to any aquarium. Its yellow color is particularly attractive, sporting a highlighted, airbrushed look. Breeding, however, is difficult because this cichlid has a tendency to eject its young at the slightest provocation.

HAPLOCHROMIS LINNI
Nimbochromis linni
Longnose Polystigma

H. linni's most impressive characteristic is a long snout. This is unique among Malawi Cichlids. It would be a tragedy, therefore, to destroy this trait through mishandled breeding. However, many *H. linni* I have seen in the U.S. don't have this distinctive snout. These fish are obvious *H. linni/H. polystigma* hybrids. The market for this fish may eventually suffer if enough inferior hybrids are injected into the industry as true *H. linni*.

HAPLOCHROMIS LITHOBATES
Otopharynx lithobates
Red Top Aristochromis

For years, *H. lithobates* has been called *Red Top Aristochromis*, even though this cichlid is *not* a member of the *Aristochromis* genus. The name became thoroughly entrenched in the United States. Identification was difficult, because this fish looked somewhat like *both* a *Haplochromis* and a peacock. The name *lithobates* has only been given to this fish recently.

HAPLOCHROMIS LIVINGSTONII
Nimbochromis livingstonii

H. livingstonii has an unusual and interesting method of hunting. It waits motionless on its side, ready to ambush any fish small enough for it to readily swallow. Commercially, *H. livingstonii* was one of the earliest cichlid imports to the United States. *H. livingstonii* is very popular. Particularly popular are the juveniles, whose color is competitive with that of the adult.

HAPLOCHROMIS MACROSTOMA
Tyrannochromis macrostoma

Although closely resembling *H. fuscotaeniatus* (p.67), *H. macrostoma* has never enjoyed *H. fuscotaeniatus*' popularity. Perhaps this can be attributed to both limited availability and the fact that few photos depict this cichlid to full advantage.

HAPLOCHROMIS MARGUERITA
Otopharynx auromarginatus

This is another cichlid that has never made a big splash in the industry, despite its vivid coloring and peaceful nature. Perhaps this is because, since *H. marguerita* take two years to reach its full splendor, breeders tend to sell this fish before it's ready. Thus, dealers receive only mediocre specimens of this beautiful cichlid.

LAKE MALAWI

HAPLOCHROMIS MILOMO
Placidochromis milomo
VC-10

This is yet another cichlid whose wild counterpart has large, fleshy lips. However, this striking feature disappears in all domestically bred specimens. This is unfortunate, as this is one of its most interesting traits. The name VC-10—the only name it possessed for years—was reportedly coined by a collector. He named it after the airplane he used when collecting this fish from Lake Malawi.

HAPLOCHROMIS MLOTO

Copadichromis mloto
Ivory Head Haplochromis

H. mloto has many admirers. This can be attributed to this fish's tri-tone color scheme, consisting of a white blaze on the forehead which—toward the back—fades into a light blue. This light blue coloring deepens into a rich purple/black body. However, beyond its beauty, *H. mloto* has much to recommend it. It's a peaceful plankton eater whose young can be kept in the same tank as adult *H. mloto* without being actively hunted.

LAKE MALAWI

HAPLOCHROMIS MODESTUS
Stigmatochromis modestus

In this book, we have identified a few fish we call "hidden treasures." *H. modestus* more than qualifies for this dubious honor. Although this lovely cichlid is an old import, the supply over the years has been virtually nonexistent. Therefore, few people have seen this fish. I believe that—if this fish could gain wider exposure and availability—its unique color scheme would captivate the market.

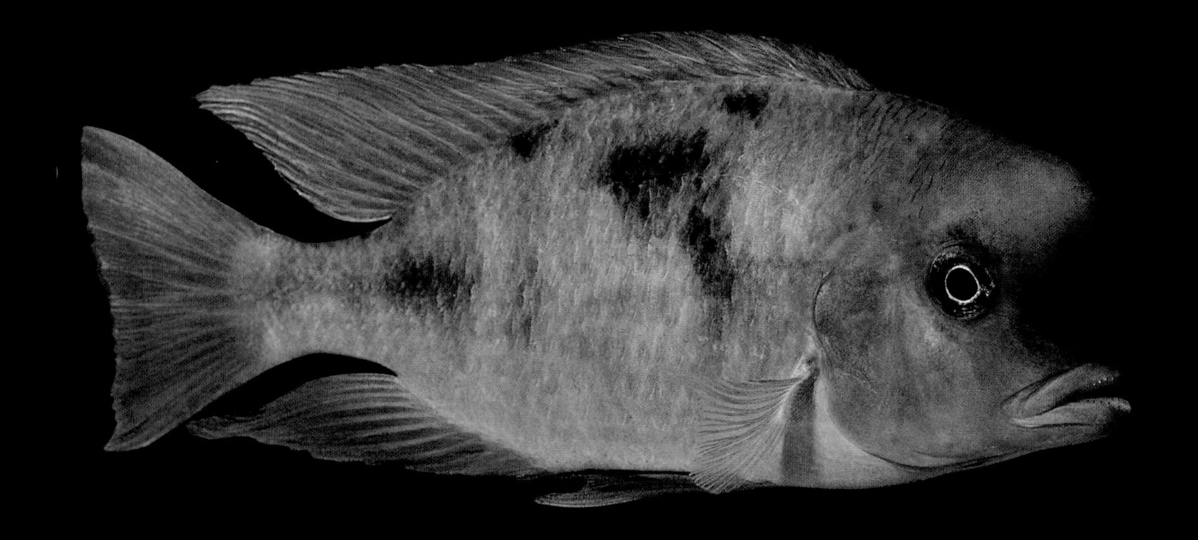

HAPLOCHROMIS MOORII
Cyrtocara moorii

H. moorii is a cichlid that has *definitely* withstood the test of time. This highly appealing fish is an early import, yet the adult still commands a high price and is in constant demand. The reasons are clear. This fish not only boasts a bright blue color, but is the only Malawi Cichlid with a distinctive hump on the forehead.

HAPLOCHROMIS MPOMBO
Otopharynx mpombo

H. mpombo resembles *H. marguerita*. It is, however, a newer import than *H. marguerita*. All *Haplochromis* that have been reclassified in the more specific *Otopharynx* genus seem to share similar large spot patterns.

HAPLOCHROMIS NDIWE
Protomelas taeniolatus (Chinyankwazi)
Fire Blue Haplochromis

The juveniles and females of *H. ndiwe* and *H. hinderi* (or *Red Empress*) are so similarly marked that they are ripe ground for hybridization. This may be the reason that there are many *Red Empresses* that are not as red as they should be. However, a little care can prevent these accidental crosses. Close examination will reveal a yellow cast to the females and young of *H. ndiwe*, while *Red Empress*' females and juveniles are pure silver.

HAPLOCHROMIS ORNATUS

Protomelas ornatus

H. ornatus **is yet** ***another*** **cichlid whose wild counterpart has a large, fleshy lip. Unfortunately, this striking feature disappears in all domestically bred specimens. Despite this, this peaceful cichlid is extremely attractive. Also, if you like large cichlids,** ***H. ornatus*** **can reach an impressive size. However, one drawback of this cichlid is that—like** ***H. flavimanus*****—it takes approximately two years to reach full color.**

HAPLOCHROMIS POLYSTIGMA
Nimbochromis polystigma

This cichlid has been a standard item in the cichlid industry since the 1970's. *H. polystigma* is mainly produced to be sold as juveniles. This fish's young have identical color as the adults. Also, like most predators, this cichlid will eat any fish small enough for it to easily swallow, but will not bother larger fish.

HAPLOCHROMIS ROSTRATUS
Fossorochromis rostratus

H. rostratus is—*by far*—the fastest and most elusive cichlid I know. This fish is highly adept at avoiding nets. Because of this, *H. rostratus* is hard to breed. Not only are the eggs very hard to collect because of this cichlid's speed, but *H. rostratus* tends to spit the eggs from her mouth prematurely. Finally, though it is a huge cichlid, *H. rostratus* is not overly aggressive toward other fish.

HAPLOCHROMIS SIMILIS

Protomelas similis
Midlined Haplochromis

H. similis **is one of the most under-appreciated cichlids on the market. This is a docile and attractive fish, boasting an exceptional number of egg spots. I believe the main reason for this unjustified lack of popularity is the number of unattractive *hybrids* passed off as *H. similis* over the years. Hybrids created through carelessness—which are less attractive than the original—have begun to sour the market for this beautiful fish.**

HAPLOCHROMIS SPILONOTUS (MAGUNGA)

Protomelas spilonotus
Haplochromis ovatus
Sulfurhead Haplochromis

This geographic *H. spilonotus* race seems to have more yellow on the forehead than many other varieties. That makes this cichlid, in my opinion, the most attractive *spilonotus* variety. However, the bright yellow blaze takes at least two years to fully develop. Most producers are unwilling to hold the fish for that length of time. Naturally, then, this fish is seldom sold when it is in full glory.

HAPLOCHROMIS SPILOPTERUS (YELLOW)
Protomelas spilopterus (Yellow)
Spilopterus Yellow

H. spilopterus (Yellow) is a mainly *blue* fish. The term *yellow* in the name refers to the underbelly. This distinguishes it from *H. spilopterus (Blue)*. The markings and shape of the *Spilopterus Yellow*'s juveniles are virtually indistinguishable from those of *H. urotaenia*. This degree of similarity is highly unusual. Breeders beware! Situations like these are where unintentional hybridizing occurs.

HAPLOCHROMIS STEVENI
Protomelas taeniolatus (Likoma)
Tangerine Tiger

H. steveni is an extremely popular fish in the cichlid world. Much of this can be attributed to its orange, striped body. This coloring makes it immediately apparent why *H. steveni* is commonly called *Tangerine Tiger*.

HAPLOCHROMIS STRIGATUS
Dimidiochromis strigatus
Sunset Haplochromis

Though a true species from the lake, *H. strigatus* looks like an *H. compressiceps*/ *H. similis* hybrid. This attractive fish has recently established an increased foot-hold in the cichlid industry.

HAPLOCHROMIS UROTAENIA
Protomelas urotaenia

H. urotaenia's yellow color is uncommon in the *Haplochromis* genus. It would be a crime—through unintentional hybridizing with *Yellow Spilopterus* (whose females and juveniles are extremely similar to those of *H. urotaenia*)—to degrade this striking feature. *Yellow Spilopterus* has significantly less yellow than that of *H. urotaenia*. A little care can prevent this degradation of a desirable trait.

HAPLOCHROMIS VENUSTUS

Nimbochromis venustus

Within the *venustus* species, there are two general color tendencies: blue and yellow. Since the yellow is less common, it would be wise to selectively breed in favor of the yellow color trait. Selecting for yellow can result in a spectacular, vibrant fish (such as in the photo). This specimen is a more compelling argument for an intelligently controlled breeding program than anything I can *write*.

HAPLOCHROMIS VIRGINALIS (BLOTCH)
Copadichromis virginalis (Blotch)

Beauty is in the eye of the beholder. I *personally* don't care for this cichlid's subtle, steel-blue coloration. However, it must be said that this color is fairly unusual. Its appearance *does* go beyond the standard silver color found in many cichlids, yet its commercial potential is questionable. However, the price may remain high due to the myriad of problems breeding *virginalis*.

HAPLOCHROMIS VIRGINALIS (CHINGATA)
Copadichromis virginalis (Chingata)
Chingata Virginalis

As of 1994, this cichlid is one of the newer imports and commands a fairly high price. However, even when domestically bred there will probably be limited availability (and thus high prices). There are, I believe, two reasons for this. First, the eggs are very large. This, of course, means fewer eggs per spawn. Secondly, this fish spawns infrequently.

HAPLOCHROMIS VIRGINALIS (GOLD CRESTED)
Copadichromis virginalis (Gold Crested)
Gold Crested Virginalis

In my experience, the *Gold Crested Virginalis*, like all other virginalis', is an infrequent spawner (even during the generally vigorous summer spawning season). This is unlike most other *Haplochromis*. Combined with its generally less popular pastel color scheme, this factor throws into question this fish's long-term commercial viability.

HAPLOCHROMIS WOODI
Stigmatochromis woodi

Until now, I had dismissed *H. woodi* as inferior. Every specimen I had ever seen was—*at its best*—a silver cichlid with black fins. However, the fish shown here is obviously different. This attractive specimen was obtained from the wild. Perhaps it comes from a different geographic location. In any case, this individual forces me to amend my position on *H. woodi*.

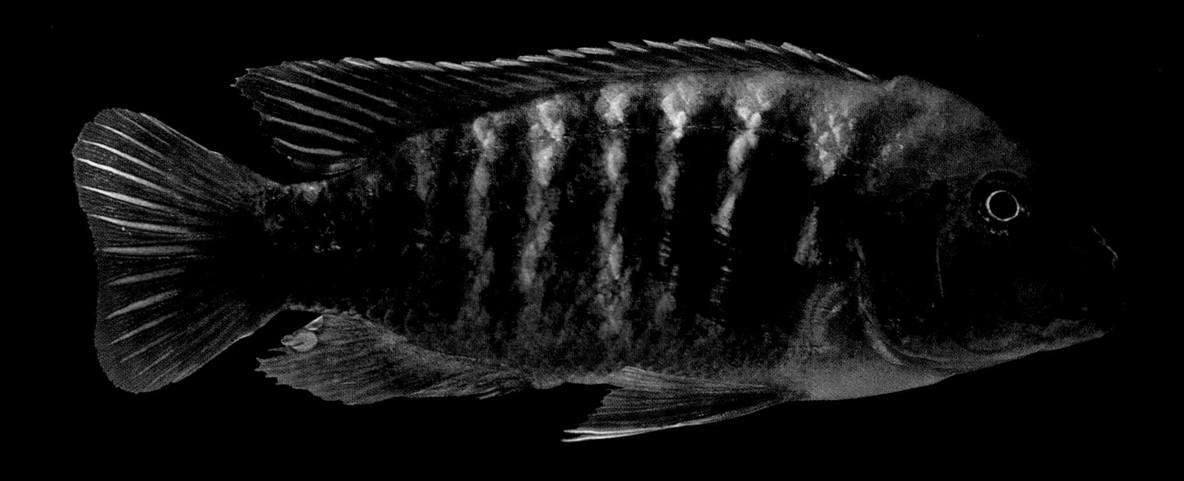

IODOCHROMIS SPRENGERAE
Rusty

L. sprengerae—commonly called *Rusty*—has been on a supply and demand rollercoaster. Since this cichlid is extremely easy to breed in large volume, many producers began to breed them. Naturally, the price then plummeted and breeders unloaded their stock. In the mid-eighties, the price began to inch back up. Since the young and adults are the same color, *Rusty* is basically sold in juvenile form.

JULIDOCHROMIS DICKFELDI

J. dickfeldi is the easiest to breed of all *Julidochromis*. A good pair of *J. dickfeldi* will be extremely prolific. However, as with all *"Julies"*, *J. dickfeldi* has a tendency to kill other members of its genus when paired. Not every male and female will mate. If a male/female pair does not *bond*, they will kill each other. This is true of all *Julidochromis*.

JULIDOCHROMIS GOMBI (TRANSCRIPTUS)

Breeding all *Julidochromis* is a delicate matter. *J. gombi (transcriptus)* is no exception. Though good parents, a mated pair of *Julidochromis* will sometimes attack each other if the fry are removed. You don't need to remove a previous spawn from the tank when a new group of fry is hatched. This is because the older young will not bother the new fry.

JULIDOCHROMIS REGANI (KIPILI)

J. regani (Kipili), in my opinion, is the most attractive member of the *Julidochromis* genus. Also, this cichlid's female is at *least* twice as large as the male. Like all *Julidochromis*, *J. regani (Kipili)* is an egg-layer. They tend to lay their eggs under objects such as flower pots. In order to successfully breed these fish, you must not disturb the object they choose as a home for their eggs.

LAKE MALAWI

LABEOTROPHEUS FUELLEBORNI (ALBINO)
Albino Fuelleborni

The *Albino Fuelleborni* was developed by a hobbyist in the United States. both the male and female shown here have albino coloring. Like many new albinos, this fish's availability is limited.

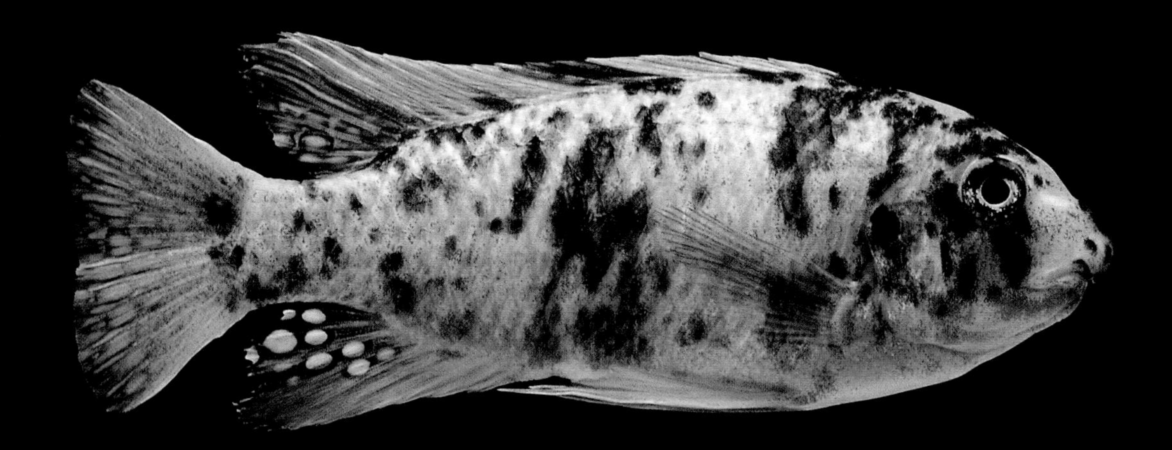

LABEOTROPHEUS FUELLEBORNI (OB)
OB Fuelleborni

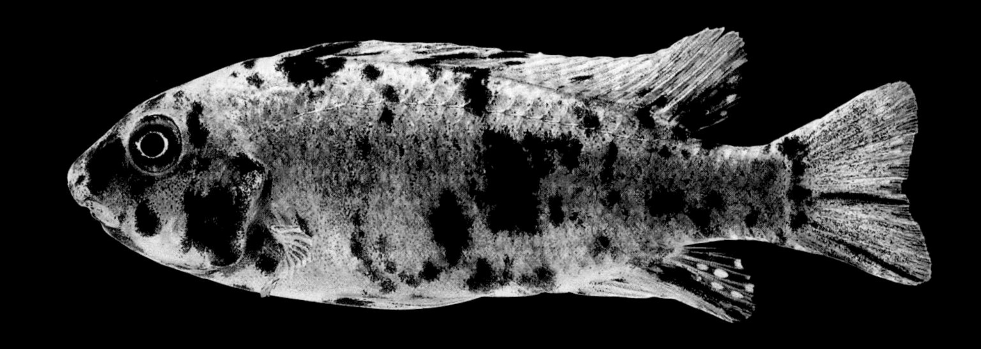

It is a common myth that the *Labeotropheus*' unique nose-like upper lip disappears after a few domestically bred generations. This is *not the case*. This is an attempt to explain away a hybridization of this fish. In the fish industry such a hybrid (commonly between a *Pseudotropheus* and a *Labeotropheus*) is called a *banana*.

LABEOTROPHEUS FUELLEBORNI (ORANGESIDED)
Orangesided Fuelleborni

The *Orangesided Fuelleborni*'s nose-like upper lip is this genus's most unique and interesting feature. Why would anyone, therefore, allow this striking trait to disappear? Yet this is often *exactly* what happens, due to unintentional hybridizing. A little vigilance can prevent this trait from fading away.

LABEOTROPHEUS FUELLEBORNI (RED TOP)
Red Top Fuelleborni

Random hybrids are seldom attractive. *Labeotropheus* are easily crossed with other fish. They are fairly indiscriminate about mating outside their genus. Therefore, this fish is fertile ground for unintentional hybrids. Again—as I've stressed many times in this book—*care* is the essential ingredient to prevent such crosses.

LABEOTROPHEUS TREWAVASAE (ALBINO RED TOP)

Albino Red Top Trewavasae

The *Albino Red Top Trewavasae* is a spectacular albino. Its pure white body combined with its vibrant, fire-engine red dorsal creates a striking, high-contrast appearance.

LABEOTROPHEUS TREWAVASAE (CHILUMBA)
Redsided Trewavasae

The *Redsided Trewavasae* is not common in the United States as of 1994. How popular this fish will prove to be in the future, I cannot say. Only time will tell.

LABEOTROPHEUS TREWAVASAE (OB RED TOP)
OB Red Top Trewavasae

The demand *always* exceeds supply for this beautiful OB morph. Because of this, the price is significantly higher than that of more common *L. trewavasae* varieties.

LABEOTROPHEUS TREWAVASAE (RED TOP)
Red Top Trewavasae

The *Red Top Trewavasae* is the most common of all *L. trewavasae* varieties. Despite this, *Red Top Trewavasae* has maintained a consistently high demand since its introduction in the 1970's. One look at the picture should make the reason obvious.

LABIDOCHROMIS CHISUMULAE
Labidochromis chisumulu

The female *L. chisumulae* is unusual. The female's striped, cream white coloring is unique among known cichlids. The male is also a desirable fish. Its pastel blue coloring creates a watercolor-like impression.

LABIDOCHROMIS HONGI
Red Top Labidochromis

Even in the wild, all fish are not created equal. Natural variation can provide the savvy breeder with an opportunity to improve his or her strain. This fish is a prime example. Starting with a fish boasting an *exceptionally* impressive yellow underbelly, a superior line of *L. hongi* can be developed. What was once exceptional can be *typical* in this strain.

LABIDOCHROMIS KAKUSA
Labidochromis caeruleus (Yellow Morph)
Yellow Labidochromis

Though from Malawi, *L. kakusa* was first domestically bred in Burundi. This fish was then exported—from Burundi—to the rest of the world. *L. kakusa* is arguably the most striking Mbuna. Its color, in fact, rivals that of many salt water fish. Predictably, it is one of the most popular cichlids in the industry.

LABIDOCHROMIS KIMPUMA
Yellow Fin Labidochromis

This attractive and peaceful fish is not readily available. However, this fish has much to recommend it. I am confident it will be increasingly popular in years to come.

LAMPROLOGUS BRICHARDI (GREEN FACE)
Neolamprologus brichardi (Green Face)
Green Face Brichardi
Fairy Cichlid

Green Face Brichardi is not as common as the standard *L. brichardi*. However, it is a more attractive fish, due to its lighter color and facial markings. *Green Face Brichardi* is a good parent. Also, fry of different generations seem able to coexist without bothering each other.

LAMPROLOGUS COMPRESSICEPS (GOLD FACE)
Altolamprologus compressiceps (Gold Face)

L. compressiceps (Gold Face), like all members of this species, is a predator. This shouldn't be a problem. Anything this cichlid can't swallow is safe from *L. compressiceps*. However, keep in mind that this species' mouth is very large in relation to its body. *L. compressiceps*' body serves it well as a predator. Its thin, leaflike shape allows it to follow its prey into narrow rock crevices.

LAMPROLOGUS COMPRESSICEPS (YELLOW CALVUS)
Altolamprologus compressiceps (Yellow Calvus)

The male of *L. compressiceps* is, on the average, three times the size of the female. This size difference allows the female to hide inside tight, narrow spaces the male cannot reach. The female does this because the male becomes very aggressive during mating season. All *L. compressiceps* are egg-layers, and the female deposits her eggs in these small, narrow spaces. Many breeders use conch shells for this purpose.

LAMPROLOGUS COMPRESSICEPS (ZAIRE BLACK)

Altolamprologus compressiceps (Zaire Black)

When breeding *L. compressiceps*, one male is generally combined with multiple females. Also, the spawn from each female is relatively large. Therefore, small specimens of this species are abundant. However, larger fish are fairly expensive, due to this cichlid's *extremely* slow growth rate. Finally, breeders must remove all *L. compressiceps* fry from the tank or the adults will eat them.

LAMPROLOGUS CYGNUS

Neolamprologus cygnus

L. cygnus is one of a small group of fish whose *juveniles* are actually *more* attractive than the adults. The adult *L. cygnus* looks fairly ordinary. However, its young are exceptionally beautiful, sporting orange and blue spots on the head and body. Because of this, most breeders produce *L. cygnus* to sell as juveniles.

LAMPROLOGUS LELEUPI
Neolamprologus leleupi

When paired, this colorful cichlid is among the more aggressive of the *Lamprologus* genus toward other members of its species. The male *L. leleupi* is at least twice the size of the female. Like *L. compressiceps*, this feature allows the egg-laying female to deposit her eggs in an area the male cannot reach. It is wise to provide a hiding place that has an opening large enough for the female but *too small* for the male.

LAMPROLOGUS SEXFACIATUS (KIPILI)
Neolamprologus sexfaciatus (Kipili)
Yellow Lamprologus Sexfaciatus

L. sexfaciatus (Kipili) has large spawns—upwards of 250 eggs. However, because the adult is aggressive toward other members of its species, it is not easy to produce. To breed this fish, provide a pot with a tile to serve as the floor, for the female to deposit her eggs on. The breeder then removes the tile, with the eggs, and hatches them artificially.

LAMPROLOGUS SPECIES (DAFFODIL)
Neolamprologus daffodil

L. species (Daffodil) looks like *L. brichardi*. However, as the name *daffodil* implies, this fish is yellow. *L. species (Daffodil)* is fairly prolific and a good parent. Also, fry from different generations don't bother each other.

LETHRINOPS MBAWA

Most members of the genus *Lethrinops* are essentially peaceful. *L. mbawa* is no exception. This trait makes *L. mbawa*—like a majority of *Lethrinops*—easy to keep and combine with other cichlids. This peaceful nature can often compensate for the lack of spectacular color in a fish.

LETHRINOPS MICRENTODON

L. micrentodon has an exceptionally deep body. Also, this cichlid's color is unusual. *L. micrentodon* has a dark blue—almost black—body with an orange nape. This coloring makes it look very much like a peacock. Together, this fish's interesting shape and odd color make *L. micrentodon* a truly unique specimen.

LETHRINOPS MICROSTOMA

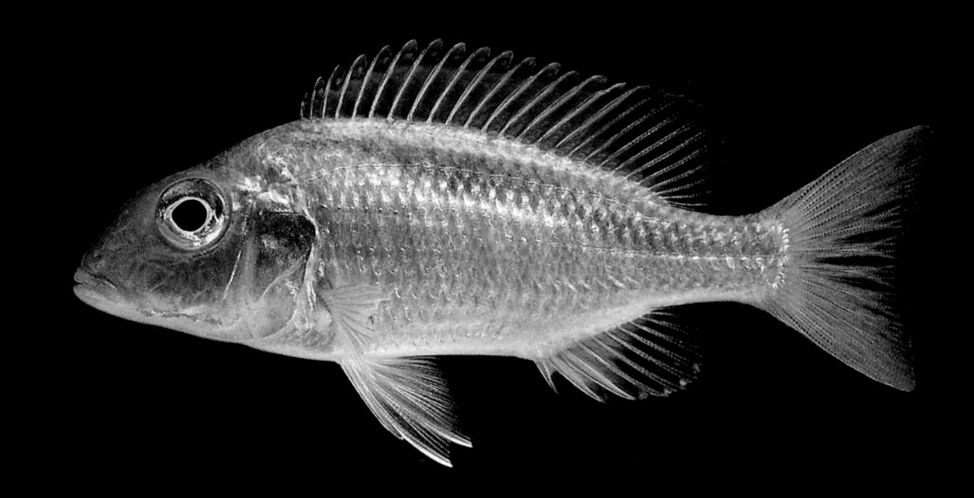

The *Lethrinops* genus possesses a distinctive and interesting shape. The heads of most members of this genus are rounded and blunt. Members of this group are bottom feeders. They sift through the sand to look for food.

LETHRINOPS OCULATUS

There are two members of the *Lethrinops* genus that are very attractive. One of these is *L. oculatus.* Intense color is an uncommon trait in the *Lethrinops* genus. Although these fish generally have subtle coloration, *L. oculatus* is an exception to the rule.

LETHRINOPS PARVIDENS
Red Flush Lethrinops

L. parvidens is the most attractive *Lethrinops*. Its bright, saturated colors stand out when compared to the muted colors common in other members of this genus. *L. parvidens'* exceptional color and rounded face make an attractive—and interesting—combination.

LETHRINOPS PRAEORBITALIS
Taeniolethrinops praeorbitalis
Lethrinops furcifer

L. praeorbitalis' fins are exceptional. The dorsal fin is very large with a sail-like shape. This fish's fins are the most vivid example of a genus whose fins—in general—are impressive. Most *Lethrinops* can boast of large and shapely fins. *L. praeorbitalis'* interesting shape and impressive finnage help compensate for its lack of color. The specimen shown here is as colorful as this fish gets.

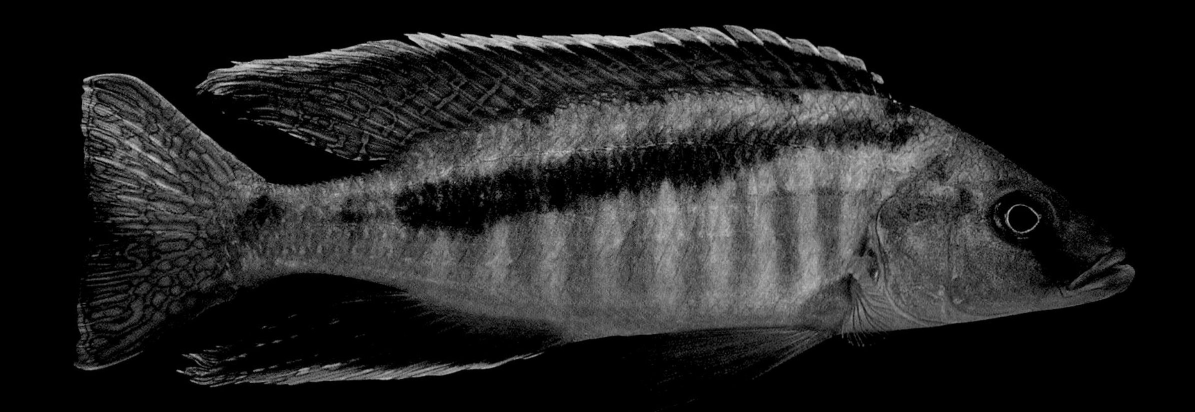

MARAVICHROMIS GRACILIS
Haplochromis gracilis
Torpedo Haplochromis

If you like a torpedo shaped, peaceful fish with intense color, *M. gracilis* is for you. Also, *M. gracilis* is presently fairly rare, especially in the United States.

MARAVICHROMIS LATERISTRIGA
Haplochromis lateristriga
Flame Oxyrhynchus

M. lateristriga looks essentially like *Hemitilapia oxyrhynchus*. However, there are several key areas where *M. lateristriga* is *superior* to *H. oxyrhynchus*. Its dorsal and anal fins are larger and more red. In addition, this fish sports a diagonal line in place of *H. oxyrhynchus*' spots. The similarities between the two are why *M. lateristriga* is commonly known as *Flame Oxyrhynchus*. In my opinion, this fish will replace *H. oxyrhynchus* in the cichlid market.

MARAVICHROMIS MOLLIS
Haplochromis mollis

This cichlid, despite being on the market since the 1970's, has never made a large impact in the cichlid world. One reason this peaceful fish may have never gained popularity is that it's not readily available. Another reason may be that it sports understated, pastel colors unlike the garish colors of many other cichlids.

MARAVICHROMIS TRIMACULATUS
Three Spot Maravichromis

Many members of the *Maravichromis* genus have a diagonal line across their bodies. *M. trimaculatus* is unique because—instead of a line—this fish has spots. In fact its name, *trimaculatus*, means "three spots". This fish is relatively docile and sports a delicate color pattern.

MELANOCHROMIS AURATUS

First appearing in the late 1960's, *M. auratus* is among the oldest of the Malawi imports. This is a standard item for anyone who keeps Malawi Cichlids. In other words, *M. auratus* is a staple of the cichlid industry. Interestingly, this cichlid's juveniles and females are more attractive than the adult male. The young have the same gold coloring as the females. Naturally, the juveniles are better sellers than the adult male.

MELANOCHROMIS AURATUS (ALBINO)
Albino Auratus

Though *M. auratus* is a common fish, the albino form is not. This variety is relatively rare as of 1994. However, large quantities will probably be available in the future. They will surely make a big splash in the cichlid industry.

LAKE MALAWI

MELANOCHROMIS CHIPOKAE

Generally, aggressive fish are not popular. However, despite its aggressive nature, *M. chipokae* has maintained a steady demand since its introduction. This can only be attributed to this fish's lovely coloring. In fact—with their horizontal black stripes over a gold body—*M. chipokae* females and juveniles are *more* attractive than the adult male.

MELANOCHROMIS EXASPERATUS

Melanochromis joanjohnsonae
Likoma Pearl

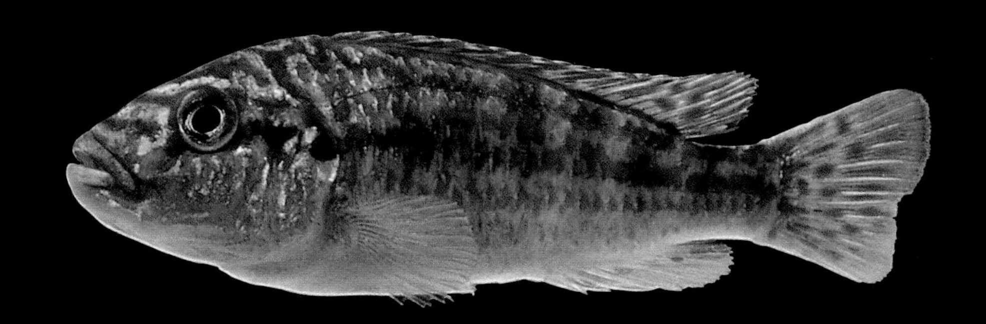

Imported in the early 1970's, *M. exasperatus* has maintained a stable presence in the cichlid industry. These fish are often sold as juveniles, which have color identical to that of the adult. This is the most peaceful *Melanochromis*.

MELANOCHROMIS JOHANNI (CHISUMULU)

This is another cichlid that is primarily sold in juvenile form. The young's rich orange color is the same as that of the female. As an adult, *M. johanni (Chisumulu)* is less aggressive than *M. chipokae*. This combination of beauty and docility make this a good seller.

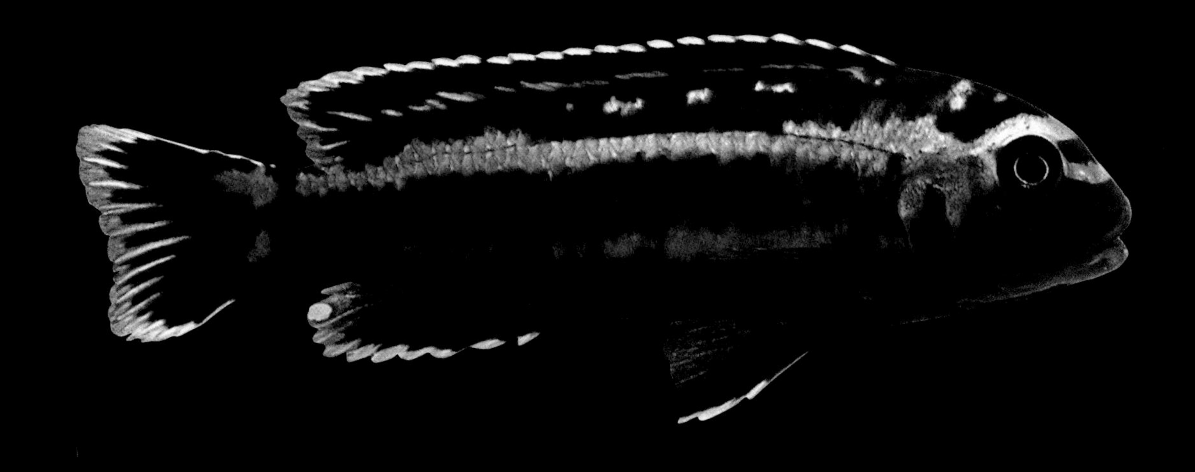

MELANOCHROMIS JOHANNI (MAINGANO)
Electric Blue Johanni

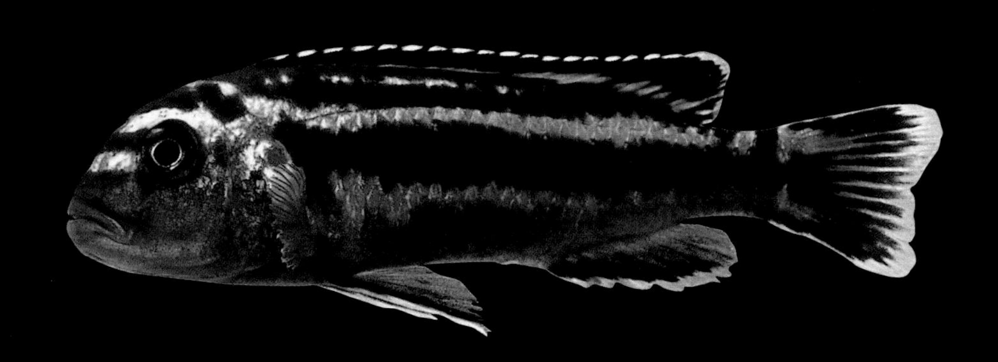

In my opinion, *M. johanni (Maingano)* is more attractive than the more common *Chisumulu* variety. In addition, the male, female and young of this cichlid look virtually identical. All of them have a rich, two-toned blue and black appearance. All of these factors explain why *M. johanni (Maingano)* is quite a bit more expensive than the *Chisumulu* variety.

MELANOCHROMIS VERMIVORUS

M. vermivorus is an early import that basically disappeared from the market until the mid-eighties, when it began to resurface. Also, this fish is not as popular as its albino counterpart. This can be partially explained by the fact that this is the least attractive of the *Melanochromis* genus.

NYASSACHROMIS HONGI

N. hongi belongs to a relatively small genus. Also, like all *Nyassachromis*, this cichlid has an elongated body. Finally, *N. hongi* is a peaceful cichlid. This is a big plus for any fish. That is why I have mentioned this trait every time it has been applicable.

TANGANYIKA

OPHTHALMOTILAPIA NASUTA (KIPILI)
Ophthalmotilapia nasuta (Orange)

This fish's most impressive feature is an *extremely* large, nose-like upper lip. This trait is significantly more pronounced in this fish than in the *Labeotropheus* genus. I'm surprised nobody has named this fish "*Pinocchio*" or "*Cyrano*". Also, this fish is docile. In fact—given a large tank with several hiding places—you can breed this fish without removing the fry from the tank. The adults won't actively hunt them.

OPHTHALMOTILAPIA VENTRALIS (BLUE)
Blue Ventralis
Mpulungu Ventralis

Like all *ventralis*, *Blue Ventralis* has long pelvic fins with a yellow spot on the tip. This exaggerated pelvic fin qualifies this fish as a member of a group commonly called *Feather Fins*. This fish's powder blue color, combined with the flowing pelvic fins, makes this a delicate looking cichlid.

OPHTHALMOTILAPIA VENTRALIS (ORANGE)
Orange Ventralis

The *Orange Ventralis* contradicts the idea that all fish of a given variety will be virtually identical. Individual members of this variety differ quite a bit—in color intensity—from one another. Also, when calm, the *Orange Ventralis* is a spectacular fish. When under stress, however, this cichlid loses virtually all of its orange coloring. If a new owner is patient, this fish's color will return as it becomes accustomed to its environment.

OPHTHALMOTILAPIA VENTRALIS (ORANGE NAPE)
Orange Nape Ventralis

The *Orange Nape Ventralis* looks very similar to the *Blue Ventralis*, except for—predictably—orange behind the head. Like the *Blue Ventralis*, this cichlid has long pelvic fins. This trait qualifies the *Orange Nape Ventralis* as a member of the *Feather Fin* group. This classification is based on a single physical trait and *is not* a true species or genus classification. In fact, members of the *Cyathopharynx* genus are also *Feather Fins*.

PARATILAPIA POLLENI (MAGNA)

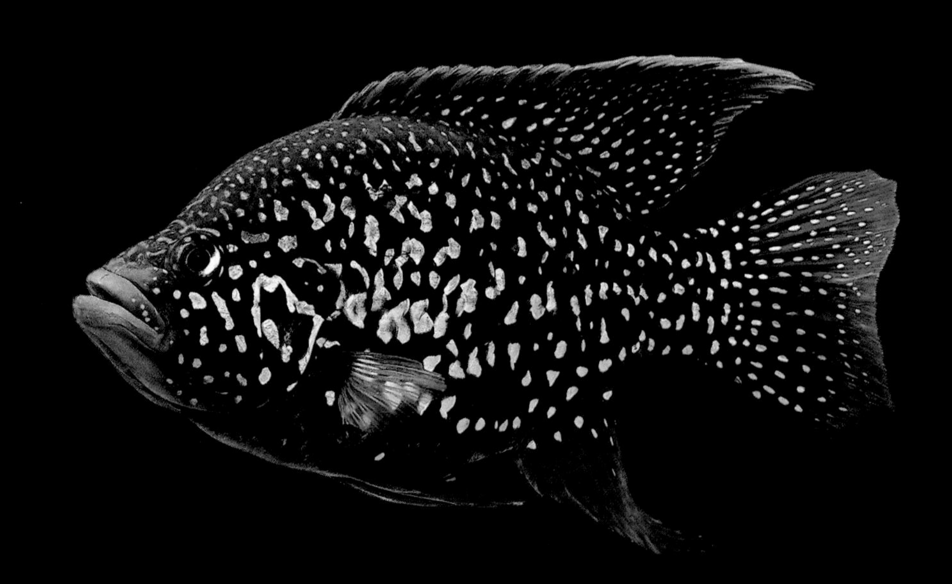

P. polleni (Magna) is one of the few cichlids to come from Madagascar. Of the limited number of Madagascar Cichlids, this is the most attractive. *P. polleni* tends to grow quite large. Also, this cichlid likes to hide in algae and buries itself—on its side—under debris when scared. Finally, *P. polleni (Magna)* produces a large spawn, yet is still a relatively rare and expensive fish as of 1994.

PARATILAPIA POLLENI (MINUTUS)

P. polleni (Minutus) is not as dark as the *Magna* variety. Its color tends to be a dark greenish brown. Also, this cichlid's spots are smaller and more numerous than those on the *Magna*-type. Both *Magna* and *Minutus* may be geographic variations of the same fish. It is important to note that the *Minutus* qualifier refers to the size of the *spots* on this variety, not the size of the fish itself.

PETROCHROMIS TREWAVASAE

P. trewavasae has an *extremely* long intestinal tract. This makes it highly susceptible to intestinal ailments if not fed properly. The long intestine implies that *P. trewavasae* is a grazer. It eats small amounts over an extended time. Its rows of tricuspid teeth are well suited to its primary diet of algae. Therefore, do *not* overfeed this fish. It is prone to bloat.

PETROTILAPIA NKHATA

P. nkhata is the most spectacular of the *Petrotilapia* genus. The male has a blue face and a body of orange/yellow punctuated by blue stripes. However, after a few years, this fish's appearance had been degenerated through random breeding. What was once a spectacular fish had been turned into a common blue cichlid. Some careless breeders allowed this trait to *disappear.* It took years to breed this fish back to its former glory.

PSEUDOTROPHEUS ACEI (TANZANIA)
Tanzania Acei

Of all *acei* varieties, the geographic race in Tanzania is, in my opinion, the most attractive. Its almost-black body and pale yellow tail fin creates a high-contrast color scheme. In addition, this fish produces small eggs. Naturally, this means large spawns. I believe that *P. acei (Tanzania)* will replace all other *acei* varieties from different localities.

PSEUDOTROPHEUS AURORA

Imported in the 1970's, *P. aurora* is—in my opinion—one of the most attractive of the *Pseudotropheus* genus. Despite this, *P. aurora* has never enjoyed much popularity because of the perception that it is an *extremely* aggressive fish. However, it should be known that many domestic strains are *less* aggressive than their wild counterparts.

LAKE MALAWI

PSEUDOTROPHEUS BARLOWI

Pseudotropheus fuscoides
Yellow Gramma

P. barlowi was first imported during the 1970's. It is a fairly colorful fish. However, it has never gained much popularity. The reason is unclear. Perhaps this lack of commercial success is due to *P. barlowi*'s chronic lack of availability.

PSEUDOTROPHEUS CRABRO

Pseudotropheus chameleo
Pseudotropheus ornatus
Bumblebee Pseudotropheus

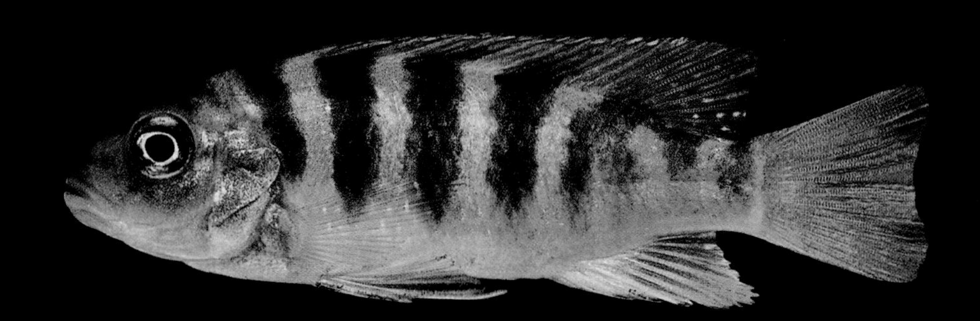

If you do not sell *P. crabro* by the time it is a young breeder, it is quite difficult to sell. While the juveniles are highly marketable, the adult male becomes fairly large—about 14 cm. (5.5 in.)—and aggressive. In addition, its color becomes muddy black. Generally, the price of a large adult male is lower than that of a young breeder.

PSEUDOTROPHEUS DAKTARI
Scissortail Pseudotropheus

P. daktari is a relatively new import, first appearing in 1992. This cichlid is the *only* fish I know that actually *looks better when raised in an indoor aquarium than when raised outdoors.* Generally, fish look better when raised outside, in a natural environment. However, when raised in an outside vat, *P. daktari* is a dull yellow. When raised inside, this same cichlid displays a bright *canary* yellow.

PSEUDOTROPHEUS ELEGANS

In my opinion, *P. elegans* is *anything* but elegant. This is a very plainly colored fish. First imported in the 1970's, *P. elegans* has never established itself in the cichlid market. One look at the photo will make the reason perfectly clear.

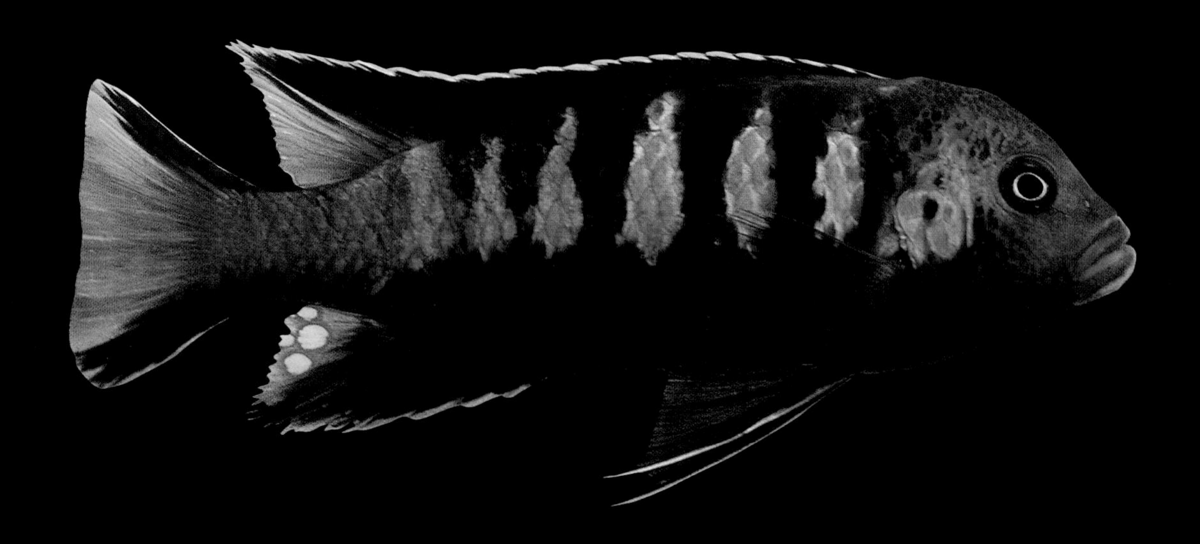

PSEUDOTROPHEUS ELONGATUS (CHEWERE)
Chewere Elongatus

Though not the most docile elongatus, I believe *Chewere Elongatus* is—by far—the most attractive of the *elongatus* varieties. The color scheme is quite vivid and the markings are crisp. Since it is a newer 1990's import, the supply for this fish is somewhat limited. A domestic strain has not yet fully established itself.

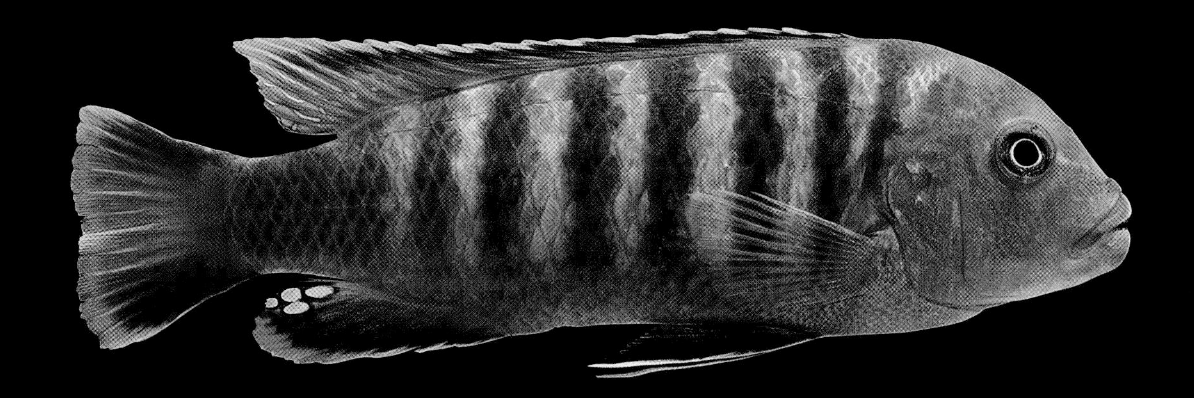

PSEUDOTROPHEUS ELONGATUS (GOLD)
Gold Elongatus

This cichlid was first imported in the early seventies as *Red Elongatus*, even though this is a mainly *gold* colored fish. The male seems to have two separate color varieties. The first variety has *Blue Zebra*-like coloring. The other—pictured here—is a blue and gold fish with brown stripes. This fish has never been popular because of its limited availability.

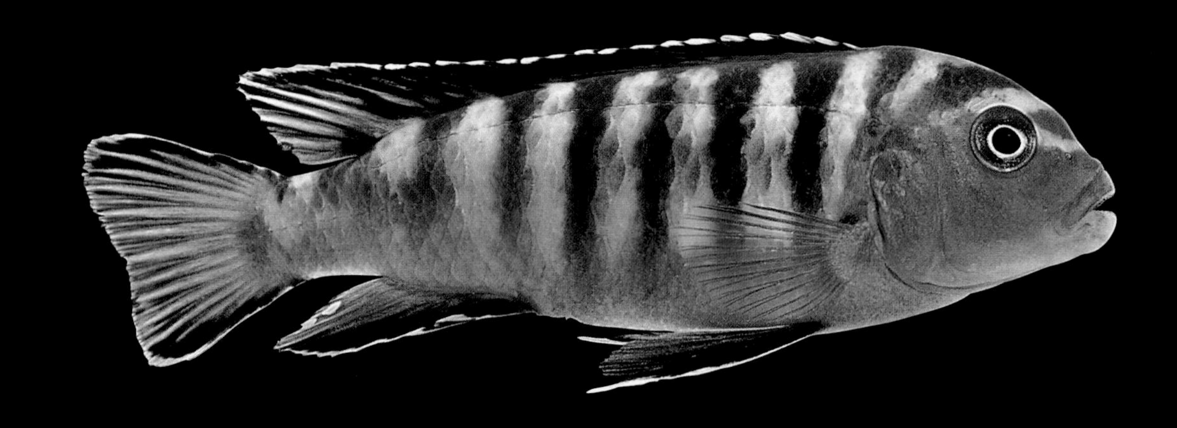

PSEUDOTROPHEUS ELONGATUS (LIKOMA)
Likoma Elongatus

In my opinion, *P. elongatus (Likoma)* is—overall—the most desirable of the elongatus varieties. There are three reasons for this. First, *both* the male *and* female are attractive. Second, the juveniles are also quite attractive, displaying the female's gold color. Third, *Likoma Elongatus* is the most docile of the *elongatus* varieties. This is particularly important, because this species tends to be aggressive.

PSEUDOTROPHEUS ELONGATUS (MBAMBA OB)
OB Elongatus (Mbamba)

The two-toned, iridescent blue spots on this OB morph are a particular stand-out. However, the standard form has a zebra-like blue body with black stripes. The female is grey. If a breeder judges an OB morph (such as the fish shown here) to be desirable, simply culling the standard male and female from the breeding stock over generations will result in a stable OB strain.

PSEUDOTROPHEUS ELONGATUS (OB)
OB Elongatus

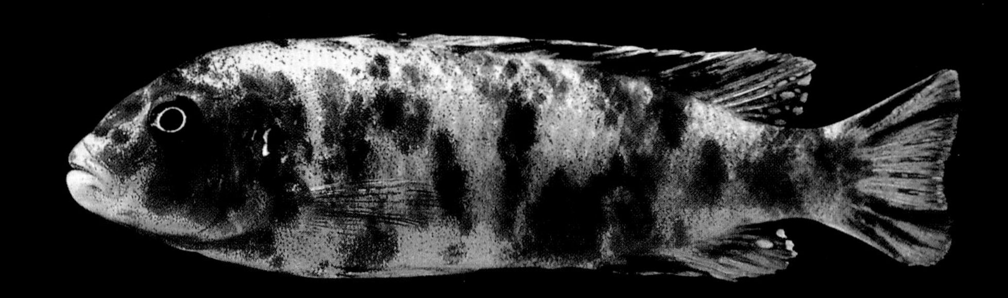

This cichlid is a spontaneous, natural mutation of a regular *P. elongatus*. This is a perfect example of how a wise breeder can *capitalize* on a fortuitous morph (resulting from the production of tens of thousands of fish). Although selective breeding did *not* play a part in the creation of this morph, selective breeding *can* prevent this trait from disappearing back into the gene pool.

PSEUDOTROPHEUS GREBERI
Pseudotropheus hajomaylandi

P. greberi **is an old import. This fish has maintained a steady demand, but has never captivated the cichlid world's attention. The juveniles of this fish are easy to sell. They are colorful relative to the young of most other cichlids. This can be attributed to their yellow fins.**

PSEUDOTROPHEUS GRESHAKEI
Pseudotropheus Ice Blue
Red Top Ice Blue

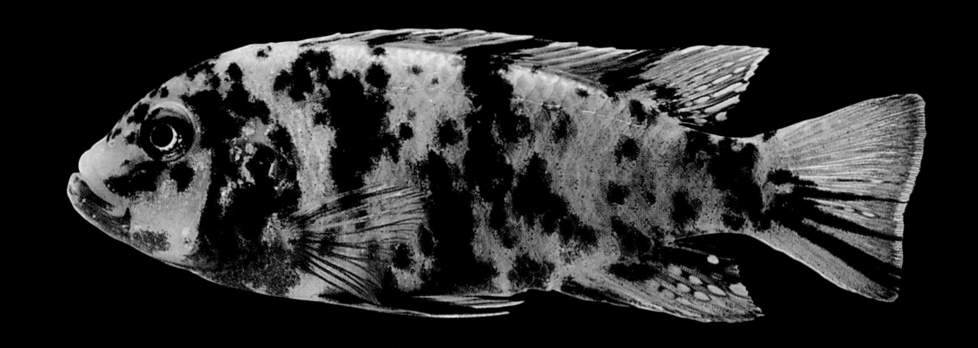

P. greshakei's flame-red dorsal and tail fins are the most intense of any Malawi Cichlid. The female shown here is an OB mutation. This means there are now two color varieties: the OB male and female, and the standard blue male with grey female. Since the OB female is more attractive than the standard variety, an intelligently controlled breeding program would take advantage of this mutation to enhance the female's color.

PSEUDOTROPHEUS GRESHAKEI (ALBINO)
Albino Red Top Ice Blue
Pseudotropheus Ice Blue (Albino)

The *Albino Red Top Ice Blue* shown above is the result of careful planning. Like the *Red Peacock*, this cichlid is an example of an engineered, man-made fish. The striking contrast between the red fins and white body make this a fish with *definite* visual impact.

PSEUDOTROPHEUS KENEI
Pseudotropheus lombardoi

From the wild, the female *P. kenei* is an attractive blue. However, this color has degenerated, via uncontrolled breeding, into a dull yellow. Instead of selectively breeding to maintain this cichlid's appearance, some careless breeders allowed the female to *lose* its original color. It took years to restore this fish's females to their former beauty. Even today, *P. kenei* often spawns undesirable throwbacks.

PSEUDOTROPHEUS MACROPHTHALMUS

Red Hood Macrophthalmus

In *Red Hood Macrophthalmus* we see yet *another* example of the power of selective breeding. The cichlid shown here was developed *solely* from the *Red Cheek Macrophthalmus*. As anyone can see, the amount of red on this enhanced specimen puts *Red Cheek Macrophthalmus* to shame. We purposely used *Red Hood*, instead of *Red Cheek*, for this strain to differentiate the two. *Red Hood Macrophthalmus* is a perfect spokesman for a controlled breeding program.

PSEUDOTROPHEUS MACROPHTHALMUS (ALBINO)
Albino Red Hood Macrophthalmus

The albino form of *P. macrophthalmus* is the only albino Malawi Cichlid—that I have seen—to come from the Orient. The original albino form, *Albino Red Cheek Macrophthalmus*, did not have large amounts of orange on its flanks. Selective breeding again entered the picture, enlarging the orange areas on the original albino macrophthalmus. This continued development led to the strain shown here: *Albino Red Hood Macrophthalmus*.

PSEUDOTROPHEUS MAGUNGA (STRIPED)
Pseudotropheus deep (Striped)

The color scheme of this relatively new import is vaguely similar to that of *P. johanni (Chisumulu)*. This cichlid, however, has a shorter, deeper body than *P. johanni*. The juveniles of this fish are very attractive. Unfortunately, as of 1994, the domestic *P. magunga (Striped)* is not available in large quantities.

PSEUDOTROPHEUS PINDANI
Pseudotropheus socolofi

P. pindani is often confused with *P. "burrower"*. The two fish look similar. However, *P. pindani* has a wide black band on the dorsal fin that *P. "burrower"* lacks. In my opinion, *P. pindani* is a more attractive fish. *P. pindani* is often sold in juvenile form, due to the young's attractive, powder blue color.

PSEUDOTROPHEUS SAULOSI

The male *P. saulosi* resembles a more intensely colored female *P. kenei*. The female of this cichlid is a saturated gold. Naturally, this fish is a viable addition to the already powerful Mbuna presence in the cichlid market. As of 1994, the price is still rather high in relation to more common Mbunas.

PSEUDOTROPHEUS SHAURI

This relatively unknown fish was first imported in 1993. Both the females and juveniles are a bright lemon yellow. The attractiveness of the young makes it predictable that—like *P. kenei* and *M. johanni*—*P. shauri's* juveniles will enjoy brisk sales.

PSEUDOTROPHEUS TROPHEOPS (BLACK TAIL)
Black Tail Tropheops

***Black Tail Tropheops*' two-toned yellow and black fins, coupled with its two-toned yellow and blue body, make this a lovely fish. However, this cichlid has a highly questionable future. This is because *P. tropheops (Black Tail)* is highly aggressive. This, of course, renders this cichlid hard to keep in an aquarium with other fish.**

PSEUDOTROPHEUS TROPHEOPS (MBAMBA)
Mbamba Bay Tropheops

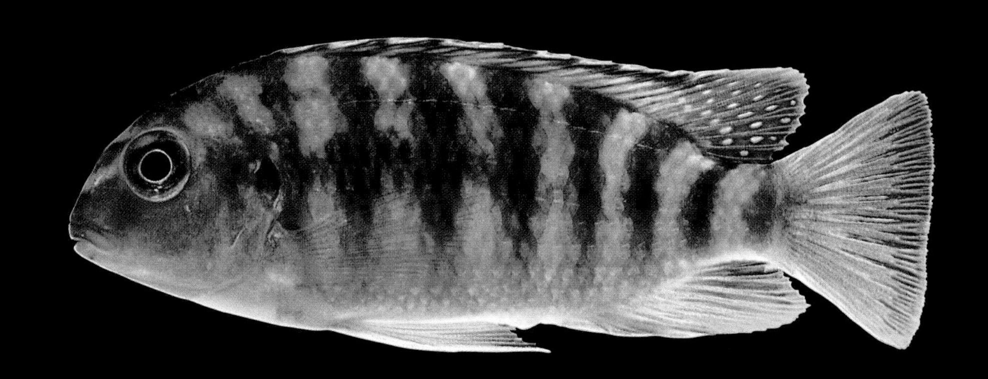

Though attractive, *Mbamba Bay Tropheops*' future is uncertain. This is because, in addition to closely resembling several other *Tropheops* varieties, this fish is relatively aggressive. Many aggressive fish fade into commercial oblivion because of this trait. Aggressiveness can *really* limit a cichlid's commercial viability.

PSEUDOTROPHEUS TROPHEOPS (POMBO ROCK)
Pombo Rock Tropheops

Pombo Rock Tropheops is another fish—like *Mbamba Bay Tropheops*—whose future is uncertain. Like *Mbamba Bay Tropheops*, this cichlid resembles several other *tropheops* varieties. This fish is also aggressive. Many fish fade into commercial oblivion because of this trait.

PSEUDOTROPHEUS TROPHEOPS (RED FIN)
Red Fin Tropheops

This cichlid is not yet fully established in the industry. As of 1994, this is a fairly new import. However, I am sure *Red Fin Tropheops* will gain a firm foothold in the industry as availability increases. The juvenile form is quite attractive.

PSEUDOTROPHEUS ZEBRA (ALBINO)
Albino Zebra

Introduced in the 1970's, *Albino Zebra* is the *first* albino Malawi Cichlid produced in the U.S. This albino was very rare when it was first available. However, *Albino Zebra* is now a staple of the cichlid industry. When attempting to produce specific traits—such as albino mutations—beware of inbreeding. Repeatedly mating fish within the same gene pool tends to create deformities and loss of vigor. It is important to frequently introduce outside bloodlines to your strain.

PSEUDOTROPHEUS ZEBRA (COBALT)

Cobalt Zebra

Cobalt Zebra has commanded a good price for 25 years. This is because, combined with this fish's bright color, *Cobalt Zebra* produces less young per spawn than many *Pseudotropheus*. Therefore, the demand always remains higher than the available supply. Because of the difficulty in breeding large volumes of *Cobalt Zebras*, this is one of the few fish that—despite being domestically bred—is still routinely purchased from the wild.

PSEUDOTROPHEUS ZEBRA (COBALT ALBINO)
Albino Cobalt Zebra

It is a good bet that this albino will *always* command a high price. The regular form of *Cobalt Zebra* is difficult to breed in volume. Combine this with an albino's less prolific nature, and you have the formula for a high demand, low supply cichlid. Also, this fish's beauty will ensure that it *remains* popular. *Albino Cobalt*'s white body is accentuated by a pearly blue cast.

PSEUDOTROPHEUS ZEBRA (GOLD BREASTED)
Gold Breasted Zebra

The *Gold Breasted Zebra* looks essentially like a *Red Top Zebra*. However, the *Gold Breasted Zebra* possesses, predictably, a gold area on its forward underbelly. This zebra is a newer import and, therefore, has not had the wide exposure of *Red Top Zebra*.

PSEUDOTROPHEUS ZEBRA (LONG FIN)
Long Fin Zebra

This zebra has earned the name *Long Fin* because, predictably, of its long pelvic fins. Overall, this fish is among the largest of the Mbunas. It can reach an impressive size of over 14cm. (5.5 in.). If you like large fish, *Long Fin Zebra* is for you.

PSEUDOTROPHEUS ZEBRA (MBENJI)
Mbenji Zebra

The *Mbenji Zebra* is among the most attractive of the OB zebra morphs. Presently, this zebra is not plentiful in the market. However, I believe it will be in high demand in the future. In the looks department, *Mbenji Zebra* has everything you're looking for—and more.

PSEUDOTROPHEUS ZEBRA (MBENJI ALBINO)
Albino Mbenji Zebra

The *Albino Mbenji Zebra* looks very much like *P. greshakei (Albino)* except that, instead of a solid white body, this zebra possesses a pinkish body with white blotches. This interesting body color, combined with the flame-red dorsal and tail fins, makes this an extremely desirable fish. However, this cichlid is not yet available as of 1994.

PSEUDOTROPHEUS ZEBRA (PEARL)
Pearl Zebra

Pearl Zebra is the *only* known non-albino cichlid in Lake Malawi that can claim solid, pearly-white coloration. This odd coloration makes it quite popular. Unlike many *zebras*, this fish produces a low number of young per spawn. *Pearl Zebra* shares this trait with *Cobalt Zebra*.

PSEUDOTROPHEUS ZEBRA (PEARL OB)
OB Pearl Zebra

The *OB Pearl Zebra* shown here is a natural mutation of a domestically bred fish. Whether this OB morph appears in the wild is not certain. Mutations are very rare. Generally, if you see *any*, it is the result of breeding tens of thousands of fish. I have noticed that among Mbunas, when mutations occur, there is a tendency toward OB (and tangerine) color mutations.

PSEUDOTROPHEUS ZEBRA (RED)
Red Zebra

The *Red Zebra* is a selective breeding success story. In the wild, blue males are common. Red males are very rare. Today, however, domestic red males are quite common. This is because most producers used the more attractive and rare *red* males for breeding. Now the red variety is more common than the blue. This is a case of breeders *intelligently* breeding their cichlids.

PSEUDOTROPHEUS ZEBRA (RED ALBINO)
Albino Red Zebra

Albinism—such as with *Red Albino Zebra*—has been appearing more often among Mbunas recently. This can be attributed to the steadily increasing volume of cichlids being produced by breeders. Of course, mutations are more likely when you produce fish on a large scale.

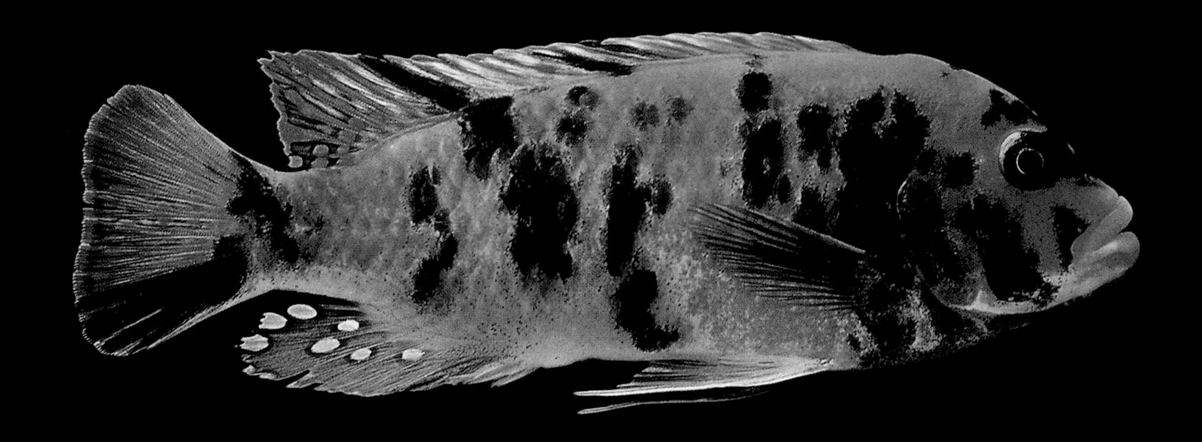

PSEUDOTROPHEUS ZEBRA (RED OB)
Koi Zebra
Red OB Zebra

This OB morph of the *Red Zebra* has an interesting life story. *Red OB Zebra* was first imported from Mozambique—in limited quantities—in 1975. However, this variety almost completely disappeared until 1990. As of 1994, this cichlid is definitely on the comeback trail. The reasons for this renewed interest are obvious. This zebra is both peaceful and *the* most spectacular of any OB morph.

PSEUDOTROPHEUS ZEBRA (RED TOP)
Red Top Zebra

The *Red Top Zebra* shown here is a product of selective breeding in two ways. First, the female is an OB mutation. Since the OB female is more attractive than its grey counterpart, it has been *purposely* favored over the standard female. The result is a strain with many OB females. Second, selective breeding has played a part in the enhanced red fins you see on the male. The best of each generation was picked to be the progenitor of the subsequent breeding stock.

PSEUDOTROPHEUS ZEBRA (RED TOP TANGERINE)
Red Top Tangerine Zebra

Tangerine color, in itself, is not that interesting. However, *Red Top Tangerine Zebra*'s tangerine body and red fins create a high-contrast color scheme, making this an eye-catching specimen.

PSEUDOTROPHEUS ZEBRA (USISYA)
Gold Zebra

Gold Zebra is a very brightly colored fish. This is among the best looking of the yellow zebra morphs. Overall, *Gold Zebra* is a commercially viable cichlid. However, very few domestic strains are available as of 1994.

RHAMPHOCHROMIS MACROPHTHALMUS

Barracuda Cichlid

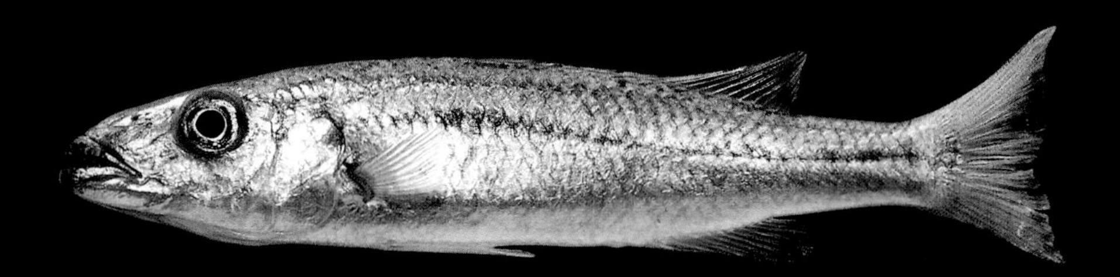

R. macrophthalmus' rocket-like shape and quicksilver color lends it a strong resemblance to a barracuda. This elegant shape compensates for its lack of color. Like a barracuda, *R. macrophthalmus* is a predator. However, this should be no problem. *R. macrophthalmus* only eats fish it can easily swallow and is not aggressive to other, larger fish.

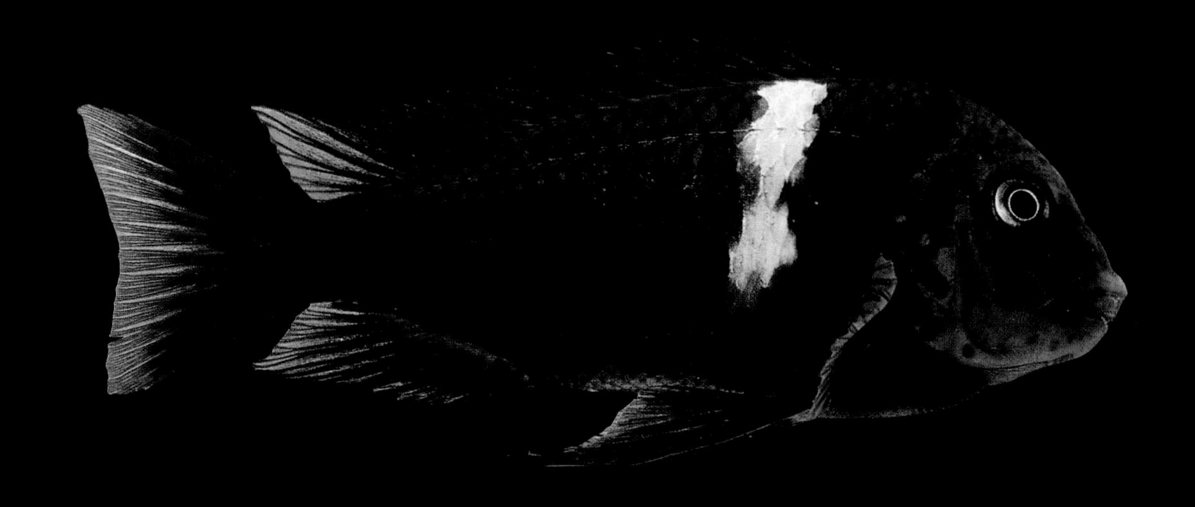

TROPHEUS DUBOISI (MASWA)

T. duboisi (Maswa) has the most black coloring of any member of the *Tropheus* genus. While the adult form is not particularly good looking compared to many other *Tropheus*, the juveniles are the *most* attractive of any produced by this genus. This is because of their jet-black bodies adorned with many jewellike white spots.

TROPHEUS MOORII (CHERRY SPOTS)
Cherry Spots Tropheus

The *Cherry Spots* variety is a typically colorful member of this species. Like all *T. moorii*, *Cherry Spots* is an algae eater. Its rounded face and upper lip, which extends beyond its lower counterpart, reveals this fish's grazing nature. *T. moorii (Cherry Spots)* eats small amounts over an extended period. Therefore, it is important not to overfeed this cichlid. A *T. moorii*'s longer intestine is more prone to bacterial infections if you feed it a large, high protein diet.

TROPHEUS MOORII (FLAME)
Flame Tropheus

Looking at the orange and red band dividing its black body, it becomes obvious why this *T. moorii* variety is called *Flame*. Like most *T. moorii* varieties, this cichlid is quite aggressive with other members of its species. However, this group of cichlids doesn't tend to bother tank-mates outside its own species.

TROPHEUS MOORII (IKOLA KAISER)
Kaiser Tropheus

One advantage of *T. moorii* is both the male and female have attractive coloring. In fact, both sexes look very similar. Generally, the male is larger than the female. However, this is not a surefire way to distinguish the sexes. Some *Tropheus* varieties' females have egg spots on the anal fin. This is the case with *T. moorii (Ikola Kaiser)*. However, this trait is not universal among *mooriis*.

TROPHEUS MOORII (MOLIRO)
Firecracker Tropheus

T. moorii (Moliro) is commonly known as *Firecracker Tropheus*. One look at this fish's overall red color is more than enough explanation. This variety is somewhat easier to spawn than most other *T. moorii* varieties. It will yield a larger number of eggs than most members of this species. However, *Firecracker Tropheus* still lays a fairly small number of eggs compared to many other cichlids.

TROPHEUS MOORII (PAPAGAI)
Papagai Tropheus

Papagai is the least common of all the *T. moorii* varieties shown in this book. However, even when a domestic strain *does* establish itself, this fish—like virtually all *T. moorii*—will remain expensive. The reason is that most members of this species lay small spawns, numbering only 10 on average. This, of course, makes most *T. moorii* high-demand, low-supply cichlids. Because of this high price, members of this species are mainly sold as juveniles.

TROPHEUS MOORII (RED RAINBOW)
Red Rainbow Tropheus

T. mooriis are not the easiest fish to keep, because of their delicate nature. These cichlids are not recommended for the beginning hobbyist. *T. moorii (Red Rainbow)* is no exception. Its long intestinal tract is susceptible to many bacterial diseases. This is especially true if *T. moorii* is fed a meaty, high-protein diet. Also, clean water seems to be more essential to this species' health than most other cichlids. However, their beauty makes it more than worth the effort.

TANGANYIKA

XENOTILAPIA PAPILIO

This 1994 import's price will probably remain fairly high over the years. This is because *X. papilio* has large eggs and, therefore, produces a limited number of fry. Also, *X. papilio* likes to dig pits in the sand when spawning. So it is probably a good idea to line the bottom of its aquarium with a deep layer of fine sand instead of gravel.

INDEX

LITERATURE

AXELROD, H.R. and **BURGESS, W.E.** (1979)
African Cichlids of Lake Malawi and Tanganyika.
8th Ed. TFH Publications. Neptune, N.J., U.S.A.

BAENSCH, H.A. and **Riehl, R.** (1993)
Aquarium Atlas, Vol. 2. 1st English Ed.
MERGUS-Verlag GmbH Hans A. Baensch
Melle, Germany.

BAENSCH, H.A. and **Riehl, R.** (1991)
Aquarium Atlas, Vol. 1. 3rd English Ed.
MERGUS-Verlag GmbH Hans A. Baensch
Melle, Germany.

KONINGS, A. (1990) *Ad Konings's Book of Cichlids and All The Other Fishes of Lake Malawi.* TFH Publications. Neptune, N.J., U.S.A.

KONINGS, A. (1988) *Tanganjika Cichliden*
Lake Fish Movies & Verduijn Cichlids
Netherlands.

VIERKE, J. (1988) *Dwarf Cichlids.* TFH Publications.
Neptune, N.J., U.S.A.